Praise for Chakr

"Special alert: David Pond's b..... ... ... it catapults the serious student into a completely transformed Self, awakening to a new reality. This broad-ranging powerhouse is the premier treatment of the subject and beyond—yes!"

—Diana Stone, author of *Playing the Ascension Game*

"*Chakras Beyond Beginners* is an insightful and uplifting gift—a true gem. David takes us on an enlightening tour of each chakra, explaining the energetic essence of who we are and making clear that when we control our energy, we control our destiny. This book is a required resource as we move forward in our human evolution. Bravo!"

—Alex Holland, MAc, LAc, author of *Voices of Qi: An Introductory Guide to Traditional Chinese Medicine*

"Anchored at the center of converging illumination, inspiration, and compassion, gifted teacher David Pond opens the way for a spiritually mature journey, embracing the depths and riches of the eternal path through the chakras. We are blessed to have such a skilled, generous guide to bless us with his profound and applicable spiritual wisdom!"

—Linda Howe, author of *How to Read the Akashic Records*, *Healing Through the Akashic Records*, and *Discover Your Soul's Path Through the Akashic Records*

"I have known and respected David for decades as a fellow astrologer, but he is also well known for his yoga teachings and spiritual seminars around the world and for his healing work with clients from all walks of life. This new offering could be considered a seminar preserved in book form so that we can refer back to it when stress gets our chakras out of alignment. If you are an astrologer or a healer yourself, you'll find techniques and new perspectives in this book that your clients can use to regain their balance and inner peace."

—Donna Cunningham, author of *Counseling Principles for Astrologers* and *The Stellium Handbook*

"Chapter One Bookstore has been selling books in Ketchum, Idaho, since 1970. Beginning with the first edition of [David's] *Chakras for Beginners* in 1999, our bookstore has literally sold hundreds of copies of this title—we call it our 'candy.' It has been our most sustainable, helpful, consistent selling metaphysical title. We are thrilled with this new publication on the chakras. David's knowledge of the chakras is what Rumi is to sacred poetry and Eckhart Tolle is to the present moment."

—Cheryl Thomas, owner/operator of Chapter One Bookstore in Ketchum, Idaho

"David Pond's newest book, *Chakras Beyond Beginners*, is timely. Human consciousness has become, more than ever before, acutely aware of the importance of one's own energy system. In our calm presence we are able to create, receive more, and live happy, balanced lives. David takes the reader on a journey, teaching new skills to deepen our relationship with our highly creative and magnetizing true selves."

—Marie Manuchehri, author of *Intuitive Self-Healing*

"As the word *chakra* continues to move into mainstream vernacular, without question this will be the go-to book for many years to come. David Pond has indeed penned both a valuable resource and a treasure."

—Andria Friesen, owner of Friesen Gallery in Sun Valley, Idaho;
author of *Speak for the Trees*; and board member of
Sun Valley Wellness Institute

"I would suggest you read the book slowly and carefully to get the full measure of David Pond's knowledge and sensitivity to the chakras as well as his gentle soul and spirit. This book has the ability to wake up people if they so wish to be. It is beautiful from the beginning and it upholds this sense of kindness, direction, and hope for change right up to the last story of giving from the heart. David has a profound way of telling, showing, living, and writing about 'a way of life' to others."

—Joan Hartzell, co-author of *Zen and Psychotherapy*

"David's done a masterful job of clarifying and grounding a complex subject! A must-read for anyone desiring to understand, know, and connect with the energies of their Psycho-Spiritual Self."

—William Smythe, MA, Somatic Therapist and Aikido Sensei

"David Pond describes the deeper theory, origin, and his intimate work with the chakras in such a profound way. Rarely are theory and usefulness so intimately combined in such a useful format, so that you can start to work immediately with your energy channels and begin to reap the insight and healthful patterns that such practices present."

—A. T. Mann, author of *Sacred Architecture, Sacred Landscapes*,
and *A New Vision of Astrology*

CHAKRAS
.... **BEYOND BEGINNERS**

© Linda Townsend

About the Author

David Pond is an astrologer, author, speaker, and international workshop leader. He is the author of six books on metaphysical topics, including *Chakras for Beginners, Astrology and Relationships,* and *Western Seeker, Eastern Paths.* David has a master of science degree in experimental metaphysics and has been practicing astrology for over thirty-five years. David consults with clients regularly, helping them work with their astrology to find a meaningful and fulfilling life and strategize through times of transition. David can be found online through his website: DavidPond.com.

CHAKRAS
BEYOND BEGINNERS

Awakening to the Power Within

DAVID POND

Llewellyn Publications
Woodbury, Minnesota

FIRST EDITION
Second Printing, 2017

Cover art: Shutterstock/108115649/© Shymko Svitlana
           Shutterstock/125523458/© Toria
           Shutterstock/168349430/© Artur. B
Cover design: Kevin R. Brown
Interior art: Figures on pages xviii and 3 by Mary Ann Zapalac;
           chakras by the Llewellyn Art Department

Llewellyn Publications is a registered trademark of Llewellyn Worldwide Ltd.

Library of Congress Cataloging-in-Publication Data
Names: Pond, David, author.
Title: Chakras beyond beginners : awakening to the power within / by David
   Pond.
Description: First edition. | Woodbury, MN : Llewellyn Publications, a
   Division of Llewellyn Worldwide, Ltd., [2016] | Includes bibliographical
   references.
Identifiers: LCCN 2016023386 (print) | LCCN 2016029602 (ebook) | ISBN
   9780738748597 | ISBN 9780738750873 ()
Subjects: LCSH: Chakras.
Classification: LCC BF1442.C53 P658 2016 (print) | LCC BF1442.C53 (ebook) |
   DDC 131—dc23
LC record available at https://lccn.loc.gov/2016023386

Llewellyn Publications
A Division of Llewellyn Worldwide Ltd.
2143 Wooddale Drive
Woodbury, MN 55125-2989
www.llewellyn.com

Printed in the United States of America

Other Books by David Pond

The Pursuit of Happiness
(Llewellyn, 2008)

Mapping Your Romantic Relationships
(Llewellyn, 2004)

Western Seeker, Eastern Paths
(Llewellyn, 2003)

Astrology & Relationships
(Llewellyn, 2001)

Chakras for Beginners
(Llewellyn, 1999)

The Metaphysical Handbook (with Lucy Pond)
(Reflecting Pond Publications, 1984)

Contents

Exercises, Practices, Contemplations, and a Heart Story

Acknowledgments

Writing a book for me is often a few-year process of bringing the original inspiration into its final form, and this book was no exception. I had been writing about the material that excites me, awakening to the power within, as a tool for my own spiritual growth.

My wife, Laurie, could see my enthusiasm and suggested I put together a book proposal. I hadn't been considering a book at that point, but I was writing about being more open to life, so I acted on her suggestion and put together a beginning outline and was working on a book proposal. It had been years since I had written a book, but on the very day I was completing the proposal, I received an email from Bill Krause, publisher for Llewellyn, asking if I had anything I was working on that I might consider publishing! Even though I was writing about the unexpected opportunities that come from being open to life, it still amazes me that the beginning of this book was one of the most powerful examples of that concept that I have ever experienced.

My four sons, Dave, Eden, Skylar, and Forest, each added valuable feedback from their unique orientations, which have improved the flow of this book. Andria Friesen went way beyond my request for her response and offered line-by-line feedback with her insightful, artistic eye. I would like to thank John Herbert for our discussions on the dream material.

I would like to thank readers Lynn Mitchell, Linda Howe-Ebright, Donna Cunningham, Diana Stone, Marie Manuchehri, Alex Holland, Cheryl Thomas, and A. T. Mann for their valuable insights.

And finally, any eloquence that could be attributed to my writing is certainly the work of my silent writing partner, my wife, Laurie, who has combed through this material several times with her meticulous eye. Thank you all.

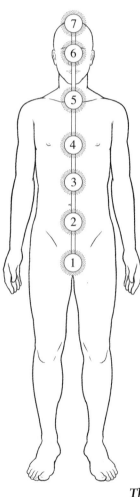

SEVENTH CHAKRA: SAHASRARA (WHITE/VIOLET)
Spirituality

SIXTH CHAKRA: AJNA (INDIGO)
Intuition/Vision

FIFTH CHAKRA: VISHUDDHA (SKY BLUE)
Truth/Expression

FOURTH CHAKRA: ANAHATA (GREEN)
Love

THIRD CHAKRA: MANIPURA (YELLOW)
Power

SECOND CHAKRA: SVADHISTHANA (ORANGE)
Pleasure/Creativity

FIRST CHAKRA: MULADHARA (RED)
Security

The Seven Main Chakras

Introduction

There is a powerful life force within you, and this is a handbook for awakening to it. This energetic core of your being is the pathway to your Higher Self, the source of the power, joy, love, well-being, clarity, wisdom, and spiritual gifts of the life you were born to live. These are the inherent qualities of your Higher Self, and they already exist within you. *Chakras Beyond Beginners* will give you keys for unlocking rooms in your consciousness so that you may experience these higher states directly within yourself.

As you learn to work with your chakras, you develop greater control over the one thing in life you can take responsibility for: your energy field. You can't control life—life is living you as much as you are living life, no matter how much you try to control it. You ultimately can't control others, nor the outcomes of your efforts, nor so many of the ups and downs that invariably come your way. However, you do have the ability to control how you respond to all that happens to you. This is your power within.

In *Chakras Beyond Beginners*, we will go beyond a basic understanding of the chakras to explore the many applications of using your chakras throughout the day to enhance the flow of vital energy in all aspects of your life. The more open and centered you are within yourself, the more the universal life force flows through you and your experience of life becomes one of "being in the flow."

Even if you are new to the chakras, you will be able to apply this information immediately in your life to experience the tremendous benefits of knowing your energetic field through your chakras and how to keep it open and balanced.

Ultimately you are the only custodian of and the final authority on your inner world and your experience of your chakras. The great value of knowing your energetic anatomy is that it is both immediate and direct. Your chakras are always with you, and you need no other resource to empower your own energy field.

As you become more adept at reading your own energy field, you become much more sensitive to and aware of other people's energy fields. Your interactions with others become enhanced as you develop your sensitivity to the subtle energy fields beyond your physical senses. Your intuition and empathy expand your ability to understand others and what they are experiencing. Your Higher Self is inherently accepting of others, and effortlessly, you become more kind in your interactions with others.

Kindness is a tonic our planet could use at this time, when pressing global problems on so many fronts are growing faster than solutions. As you learn to balance and come into greater harmony with your own energy field, by way of sympathetic vibration, even your silent presence has a centering effect on others.

For the sake of clarity and simplicity, we will distinguish between your *Personal Self* and your *Higher Self,* and they both will be capitalized throughout the book. Your Personal Self, most often called your *ego*, dwells in your lower chakras, while your *Higher*

Self resides in your upper chakras (see figure). Your Higher Self has been there all along; however, it is most often drowned out by the demanding voices generated from your lower chakras and their seemingly constant need for attention.

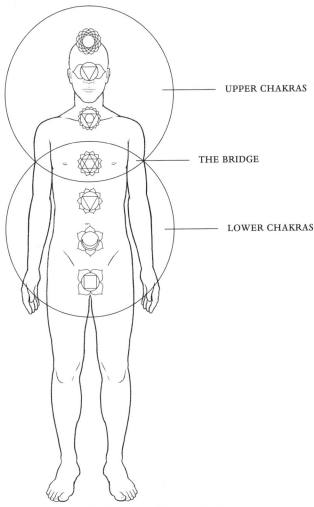

UPPER CHAKRAS

THE BRIDGE

LOWER CHAKRAS

The Upper and Lower Chakras

Your lower chakras are vital aspects of your personal life and are not to be considered negative in any way, nor are they to be done away with. It is more like your lower chakras are young puppies that your Higher Self must train in order to have any peace of mind! Your lower chakras are adorable, loving, playful, and affectionate and can add so much to your life. They are also messy and in need of constant attention and are always demanding more treats, and unless they are trained, they can bring as much trouble as good.

As you work to bring your lower chakras into balance, a healthy approach is to think of their voices in your psyche as young pups. Your personal chakras define much of your personality—your likes and dislikes, how you care for your body and the ultimate impact these habits have on your health, and how your personality asserts itself in the world.

Your Higher Self carries the qualities of your upper chakras of loving-kindness, compassion, intuitive insight, vision, and spiritual wisdom.

You grow up in a particular culture or subculture that guides you on an external path of finding fulfillment, security, and happiness. By working with your chakras, you learn how to live within yourself first. This is not an external search to acquire the quality of life you wish, but an internal quest to experience fulfillment directly within yourself.

This internalization is the direct path to what you seek. An external approach is revealed in this statement: "I will feel secure when I get the right job and get my finances in order." In *Chakras Beyond Beginners*, you will learn how to experience the security you seek directly within yourself, allowing you to make the right choices about career and financial matters from the place within you that is already secure and is not seeking security. This inside-out approach works with all of your chakras and follows this teaching from Matthew 6:33: "Seek ye first the kingdom of God, and his righteousness, and all these things shall be added unto you."

The first great benefit of following the direct path of working with your energy and allowing more of the universal life force to flow through you is that you start to become more at ease with yourself and life. By learning how to balance your energy field within, you go through life without running into as many snags and obstacles. Experiences begin to flow through you without you needing them to fit with some mental image of how you think the world should be.

The energy current flowing through your chakra system is often described as a river of energy, or *prana*. It flows from the universal life source through your crown chakra, down through the central energy channel and through each of the chakras, and ultimately out into the world through your senses. As you work with your chakras, you develop the ability to move within this river on the return current to your upper chakras, your Higher Self, and your connection to the universal source energy. To go up the river requires you to stay in the central channel of the current in order to avoid the snags near the banks that impede progress. Freedom is the ability to move at will within this river, and the snags are the things in your life that you get stuck on, hindering your ability to freely navigate the river as you choose.

Awakening to your full potential is not as much about achieving the higher states of consciousness afforded by your upper chakras as it is about removing the blocks and obstacles that inhibit the natural flow of your energy to these higher states that most certainly exist within you.

Your Personal Self resides in your lower chakras and generates your awareness of being a separate, individual entity, different from everybody else—in a body that is separate and unique from all others and is experiencing life differently than all other people. This is the realm of your ego, which is at home in your first three chakras, knowing its way around the realms of consciousness that they generate.

Your ego is the keeper of your personal story that your lower chakras will remind you of every day. A healthy ego creates a healthy story and is necessary to successfully navigate the currents of the first three chakras—its domain where it rightfully rules as lord and master. Without the personal identity that comes from your ego, you wouldn't even know where to go home tonight, let alone develop a personal life, so we never want to think of the ego as a bad thing that should be eliminated.

However, how does your ego react when you hear the call of your Higher Self to make the return journey up the river to its domain in the upper chakras? Your ego has no control beyond the lower chakras, and it will sound every alarm imaginable to convince you not to venture beyond its domain. Imagine how your "puppies" would respond to seeing you walk out the door and leaving them behind, even after all their essential needs have been met. Your ego will put up just as much resistance to you leaving it behind: "You don't know what's upriver; it could be very bad." "You have everything you need right here." "If you're not in control, you will be at the mercy of others." "You're going to lose everything you have." And on and on.

But still your Higher Self beckons, and as you surrender to its call, you discover quite a paradoxical truth: by letting go of your ego's fears about not getting what it wants in life, you get everything your ego would have wanted and so much more. Letting go of your lower chakras' grasp on your consciousness opens you up to new experiences, growth opportunities, and life itself.

Your chakra system provides an exquisite map of the seven levels of consciousness that you have available along the river of your energetic core. Each chakra filters your perspective according to its particular orientation to life, as if you were looking through various colored lenses, with each chakra coloring your perspective through its particular filter. Ideally you have the freedom to move, experience, and express yourself at all the levels of consciousness that each chakra generates.

You begin by becoming more and more aware of all the many and subtle ways you close your energy field throughout the day, and in these moments, *you choose to stay open*. In many ways, it is that simple: when you are open, you are in the flow; when you are closed, you are not. As you become more familiar with the flow of being open, you will immediately notice the constricted energy of being closed and learn which chakra is closing and what you can do to keep it open.

When you learn how to play an instrument, first you learn how to sound each individual note clearly and then you practice scales, with individual notes in succession. After you develop some command of your instrument, you want to play music. The student gives way to the musician, and then instead of studying your instrument and how to skillfully play each tone, your interest shifts to the music you are playing.

Becoming familiar with your chakras and working with them is much the same process. First you need to know the tone and range of expression of each of your individual chakras, and then you practice going from one chakra to another, up and down the scales of your energetic being. In living life, however, your chakras operate as a system rather than independently; all of your chakras are playing their music together, with all of their blended tones influencing each other, making up your energetic aura. Is the music of your being a cacophony of disjointed tones, some squeaky and some too loud? Or is it a symphony of harmonious tones resonating with each other? This is up to you, the conductor of your energy field.

As you gain more mastery in working with your chakras, you awaken from the illusions and anxiety created by identifying yourself only with your mind and its ever-changing thoughts. Awakening happens by shifting your attention from that which is constantly rising and falling in your consciousness to your awareness itself. *Shift your attention from what you are currently aware of to your awareness itself.*

Awakening isn't necessary to become aware of your lower chakras and the call of your body and your Personal Self's needs. Your body's needs, the hunger for sensory gratification, and the drive to get your needs met will all call your attention to your lower chakras each and every day. The lower chakras are where we all start. Working with your lower chakras isn't as much about awakening to them as it is bringing them into balance by taming and training their energies. This liberates your consciousness from their distractions to explore the realms of your Higher Self.

Awakening to your upper chakras is becoming aware of a different order of life beyond the separateness that is experienced from your lower chakras. *The lower chakras always, always, have an orientation of incompleteness.* "If I just had a little more of this, or less of that, or achieved something, then I would be satisfied." This grasping nature of the lower chakras and their basic sense of dissatisfaction with the way things are drives the "I want" creature inside. Even moments that are delightful are only delightful for a moment and then are gone, and your ego gets very disappointed with this, often dwelling on how things were back in the good ol' days.

Your Personal Self, the composite energy of your first three chakras, is very protective of and defensive about its story and is the source of many a soured evening. You could have experienced a delightful evening with friends that may have been 99 percent enjoyable except for one thing that was said, and your ego will dwell on that one thing that didn't make it through its defenses for hours on end, dismissing all that was enjoyable. As you learn to reside more in your upper chakras and simply observe this phenomenon going on within you, it creates a little space between your Higher Self and your reactive ego. You are able to watch the reaction without identifying with it, and it quickly passes.

As a writer, I have learned the tremendous value of getting feedback and editorial input from others, and my first litmus test is my wife, Laurie. Our minds tend to complement each other; where I tend to make intuitive leaps in my writing, her more analytical mind looks for how everything connects and the practical applications for it.

When I share my writing with Laurie, I know myself well enough to expect my lower chakras to first react defensively when she questions something I've written. I've been working with my chakras for over forty years, and still the lower chakras persist in their defensive reaction and I find myself arguing in favor of what I wrote, attempting to convince her of its merit. It happens. But I know this is going to happen, and I have learned to sit on my defensive reaction, give it some time to run its course, and then consider the merit of her feedback, which often proves invaluable. While I'm giving my defensive reaction the necessary time to run its course, I remind myself that I won't have the luxury of explaining what I have written to every reader, so I might as well move on to the task of incorporating the feedback and connecting the dots of my ideas in ways that pass this first litmus test.

From your first three chakras, you see life from your ego's perspective, separate from the world. As you awaken to your upper chakras and your Higher Self, you gain access to increasing states of interconnectedness and levels of consciousness that are common to all of humanity.

Sometimes it is not all that easy being a human, say, compared to being my dog. When I am struggling with one thing or another in my life and I notice my dog's ease in coping with her life and how readily she returns to her loving heart, it makes me wonder, *why is it so much harder to be at ease as a human and to readily return to my loving heart?* Obviously the complexity and range of our human consciousness, and having free will to navigate as we choose within this vast potential, adds to the degree of difficulty. You are not an automaton hard-wired to only react to life. Free will gives you the ability to choose how to react and direct yourself in the vastness of human consciousness. From this complexity of being rises many drives, needs, hungers, desires, and interests, all competing for attention. Thankfully, the chakras provide a map, a bigger picture, to keep it all sorted out and in perspective.

How to Use This Book

In this book, a chapter is dedicated to each chakra, identifying its qualities, attributes, and areas of influence in your life. Techniques for identifying the blocks and obstructions that inhibit the energetic flow of each chakra will be covered, as well as methods for removing these obstacles. Exercises, activities, and meditations are included to help you bring each chakra to its full potential. For those interested in yoga, postures that can help activate and balance each chakra are presented; however, practicing yoga postures is not a requirement for working with your chakras.

Perhaps you are drawn to focus on a particular chakra because of difficulties in a specific area of your life. If you are having difficulties in relationships and are rightfully drawn to work on your heart chakra, remember that all of your chakras function together as a system; problems in one chakra can stem from difficulties in another. For example, you could work on getting your heart chakra clear and still experience difficulties if your problems in relationships stem from insecurity, which is a first chakra imbalance. Getting centered in your security chakra would remove the blockages that are manifesting as being clingy and dependent in your relationships.

My Chakra Credentials

I first became interested in the chakras when I was drawn to the practice of yoga in the late 1960s, the chakras being an integral component of the yogic teachings. I have been actively involved with both ever since as the most direct path to my Higher Self and all of its many wonders. My day job, since the mid 1970s, has been working as a professional astrologer, often using the chakras to help explain a particular astrological pattern revealed in the client's chart. I use the chakras because people have direct experiences of these energetic states whether they know the language or not, and this often facilitates their understanding of astrological patterns being discussed.

I have conducted hundreds of workshops and trainings on utilizing the chakras in daily life and have worked with thousands of clients, helping them apply this system of knowledge to their real-life issues. I have seen how the chakras are actually working in people's lives. This book is an offering of what I have learned from these experiences.

I have written a number of books on various metaphysical subjects and hold a master of science degree in experimental metaphysics. Of all the many metaphysical and spiritual paths I've explored, I have found my understanding of my chakras to be the most useful and direct path to connect with my Higher Self. Whatever your life path might be, awakening to the tremendous power within you by understanding your chakras will open you to this life force and will empower all that you do.

It is in this spirit that this book was written. May we each come into greater balance and harmony within our own lives, and may this have a ripple effect and spread out into the world.

CHAPTER 1

Keys to Working with Your Chakras

There are a few key principles for approaching your work with your chakras that are instrumental in ensuring success. These core principles are as follows:

1. An inside-out approach to life
2. Cultivating your Observer level of awareness
3. The manifesting power of attention
4. Maintaining balance
5. Using breath and attention for working with the increased energy that comes from awakening to all of your chakras
6. Kundalini
7. Using a chakra journal

An Inside-Out Approach to Life

To utilize your chakras is to understand and apply the principle of an inside-out approach to life. This is reversing the futile attempt to find what you want in life by getting the world to conform to your desires. An inside-out approach recognizes that all your worldly problems can be traced to imbalances in your chakras, and by bringing your experience of energy into balance within yourself, life begins to coalesce around this centered energy and flow again.

When you take an inside-out approach to life, you first seek to make adjustments within yourself at the onset of any difficulty, rather than attempting to get the world to change. Working with your chakras gives you a way to fine-tune your experience of energy, but it is always inner work. It is empowering to look for an inner solution to outer difficulties, although this puts you in a bit of a predicament. On the one hand, this approach implies that everything is your fault; but on the other, everything is yours to control to set things right.

The Observer Within and the Seat of Awareness

Being firmly established in the detached perspective of the Observer within is essential for all work with your chakras. The Observer is the receptive mode of your sixth chakra, your spiritual eye at the center of your brow, which is normally masked over by the busy traffic of the mind. The Observer is the place within you that is aware of your thoughts and therefore not your thoughts, aware of your body and therefore not your body, aware of your emotions and therefore not your emotions. Your Observer is the seat of your awareness, the point in your consciousness that is aware of what you are experiencing even while you are experiencing it.

To help identify the Observer, which is also called the Witness, consider the place within you that is aware of when you are in a foul mood. Your awareness is not in a bad mood; it is simply observing another part of you that is.

The Observer resides in your sixth chakra and is strengthened through meditation and mindfulness training as you learn to sit quietly in peaceful awareness as the observer to all your thoughts and emotions as they come and go. This will be explored further in chapter 7, but even at the start of your work with your chakras, it is your Observer and the inner vision of your third eye that allows you to visualize and experience the subtleties of your energy field.

Exercise

. . . .

"Catch and Release" Meditation

Sit in quiet meditation with the intention of quieting your thoughts. Take a few deep breaths, relax your body, and just sit quietly. Your practice is to just watch the process of your mind. Without you even intending it, thoughts will arise. When you catch yourself holding on to one of these passing thoughts, release it. Catch and release. Watch the words of the thought form, see where your energy is drawn, and release the thought. You can't stop thoughts from emerging, even from the Observer, but this practice will help you quickly release your attention from them.

. . . .

That Which You Pay Attention to Grows

You might ask, "If all of these faculties that the upper chakras represent are already here within me, why am I not more aware of them?" Attention is the answer. Attention is everything in understanding how your chakras are manifesting, or not, in your life. The principle of *that which you pay attention to grows* becomes abundantly clear as you become more aware of the manifesting nature of your attention. Your attention is your ability to direct your life force—where your attention goes, your life force flows. If you pay attention only to the distracting voices of your lower chakras, your life will reflect the hungry, grasping characteristics of their nature. By also directing attention to your heart, your soul, and the spiritual aspects of your life, your upper chakras begin to blossom, awakening your spiritual faculties of compassion, intuition, inner vision, and spiritual illumination.

"Pay attention" is such a wonderful idiom. To pay is an expense or an investment. There is an energetic cost or investment associated with the use of your attention, and you begin to weed out the thoughts that deplete your energy, choosing to invest your attention in that which enhances your energetic field.

As you gain mastery of your ability to direct your attention, you are no longer pulled around by the vagaries of whatever your attention gets distracted by when given free license to react to whatever captures its fancy. It is as if the switch to the light bulb of your higher consciousness is turned on by your attention. The light of your higher consciousness is always there, potentially strong and bright, but without the current of your attention, its illumination remains dim.

Exercises such as visualizing and contemplating each of your chakras sharpen your ability not only to read the energetic state of each of your chakras and determine what they need for healthy expression, but also to direct your attention to the light of your Higher Self. It's hard to understand something if you are not aware of it, and by directing your attention to each of your chakras, you begin to have a better understanding of how they operate in your life, and the latent qualities of your upper chakras begin to manifest in your life.

Basically, you are adding your manifesting power to what you pay attention to. If you want more heart in your life, pay attention to what you love, not to what you think you may need to feel love. *Focusing on what you think you need empowers the need, while focusing on what you love empowers love.* Our ideas of what we expect set us up for disappointment; we are in a relationship with an idea, not the truth of the moment. Moving away from the idea and directly to the truth of the moment is the key to bringing you back to the present.

Balance

As you continue working on enhancing the energy flow of your chakras, their spinning vortices of energy essentially spin faster, and your skill at maintaining balance becomes the critical factor in your ability to sustain the increased energy. Just as a gyroscope spinning around its axis increases in ability to stay balanced as its spin increases, staying balanced in a busy life requires aligning with your axis.

A chakra that is in balance is neither diminished nor excessive in its expression. *When you are out of balance, your skewed energy*

field carries a charge that attracts situations reflecting this imbalance.
When you are balanced, your energy field is neutral, carrying neither a negative nor a positive charge, and you simply don't bump into as many things, allowing life to flow smoothly.

The mind, which creates imbalances, can't resolve the imbalances. The solution is to drop into another level of your being that is centered in accepting the as-is-ness of life, including the never-ending ups and downs. Drop into your heart and orchestrate all of the changes going on in your life from there. Thinking you will be able to get to your peaceful heart once all of the challenges of everyday life get resolved just won't happen; better to get into your centered heart first to deal with the never-ending challenges of life.

Awakening Is Always Attended with Increased Energy

Moving from any of the constricted states of resistance stemming from the lower chakras releases the energy it took to maintain the constricted state. When you let go of the resistance attending any constricted state and just let the energy be, you get the double benefit of no longer expending your energy in resistance while simultaneously becoming open to a new level of available energy, which is often experienced as an energy surge.

The surge of energy that comes from awakening to new levels of consciousness of the upper chakras can at first be experienced as an energy overload—too much energy for the established circuitry of your lower chakras to handle.

The first three chakras are all oriented toward acquiring energy directly through the physical world, with food, rest, and sensory stimulation being the sources of vitality. When you get surges of energy from the upper chakras, which are not dependent on material fuel and draw directly from the universal life force, these downloads of prana can cause anxiety, as there is no explainable reason for these energy surges that your mind can be comforted with. Until you develop vehicles of expression for the increased energy above the first three chakras, the energy is just more than what your lower chakras can handle. Eating and sleeping patterns can get disrupted, and if you haven't developed skills for dealing with these surges, anxiety attacks and even a sense of panic can set in.

Energy Follows Breath

The first secret of working with these anxiety-causing energy surges isn't a secret at all: it is breath. Anytime you are anxious to the point of feeling like you are about to burst, check your breath. It will always be tight, shallow, and constricted. Always. Knowing that energy follows breath, breathe deep into your belly, then expand your sense of self on the inhalation to accept, embrace, and encompass the energy. Slowly exhale and be with the energy.

Imagine you are a surfer facing a huge wave that is approaching. There wouldn't be any point in attempting to quiet the wave to make it more manageable. The wave is a wave, and you either rise up to ride it skillfully or get knocked silly by the overpowering force.

Use this image of the surfer with your breathing. After breathing deep into your belly a few times, on a long, slow inbreath picture yourself rising up on top of this energy wave. Expand yourself to embrace this energy, and on a slow, deep exhale, ride the energy wave and be with it. This is when you want to have an idea journal around, because when you are with this quickened energy, your intuition heightens and it is not uncommon to get flashes of insight.

Don't let these flashes of insight and innovative ideas become like whistles on the wind, disappearing as fast as they arise. Assuming you will get back to these flashes at a more convenient time doesn't usually work. If you didn't think it up the first time, how are you going to think it up later? Writers, creative people, and entrepreneurs learn the value of jotting down a few seed ideas from a flash of insight the moment it arises to avoid the aggravation of letting great ideas get away.

Kundalini

Kundalini energy rests like a coiled serpent at the base of your spine. Kundalini is the dormant potential life force energy lying asleep in the first chakra. Through breathing practices, you are able to withdraw your awareness from your senses and your mind's thoughts and awaken the sleeping coiled serpent and make way for it to rise in the spinal column, the *sushumna* channel. As your kundalini energy rises, it passes through each of your chakras and awakens human potentials lying dormant until activated.

Staying mindful of these key principles of following an inside-out approach to life, cultivating awareness of the Observer within, and using attention and breath to work with increased energy will ensure a healthy and successful journey through your chakras.

Chakra Journal

As you read about each of your chakras, you will likely get many insights from your Higher Self as to how your chakras are working, or not working, in your life. It would be helpful to keep a chakra journal by your side as you read through the material to record your insights into how you can use your chakra awareness to benefit you in your life. Just reading through the material on the chakras in this book will stir memories of instances in your own life that are related to the information and will awaken insights into how you can be more open in your life. Keeping a record of these flashes of insight you receive from your Higher Self will be a valuable resource on your path of self-discovery through your chakras.

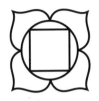

CHAPTER 2

First Chakra: Muladhara

Location: Base of the spine

Element: Earth

Symbol: A square within a circle and four lotus petals

Color: Red

Principles: Survival and security issues

Key Benefits: Feeling grounded in your body and secure in life

Key Obstacles: Fear, inherited family wounds, and imprints from childhood

Spiritual Qualities: The principles you stand on as your spiritual ground

Types of Intelligence: Instinctual, physical

Your first chakra is located at the base of your spine and is your connection to the earth and your physical body. Also called the root chakra, it is your base of operations for being in a body that is rooted and grounded in the earth. It is the most instinctual of all the chakras—it is your survival center and your connection to your primal animal nature. Your body's need to survive fuels its instinctual drive for adequate food, clothing, and shelter, fulfilling the psychological need to feel safe and secure. Your survival chakra allows you to survive a loss and live again and to bounce back after defeats and traumatic events with strong resiliency.

It is important to see the beauty of your first chakra in its own right. This chakra is not inferior to the upper chakras; it is the healthy base that is necessary to support the whole system. We don't see or focus much on the foundation of a house, our attention being drawn to the more attractive living areas above—that is, unless the foundation becomes problematic. If it crumbles, activities from the upper floors will be disrupted. The first chakra is not less important than the other chakras, but is perhaps less glamorous.

This chapter explores your first chakra's connection to your physical body, where you live, survival and security issues, as well as subconsciously stored information from early childhood and past-life karma. There will be sections on difficulties that you may have with these issues, as well as how to resolve them. Activities you can engage in to empower your first chakra can be found at the end of the chapter.

The Sanskrit name for the first chakra is *muladhara*, from the words *mula*, meaning "root," and *adhara*, which means "support" or "base." Thus, this chakra is what you need to support yourself to feel rooted and secure. With a strong root chakra, there is a feeling of being grounded in your body, with abundant physical vitality and stamina. Being balanced in the first chakra leads to having trust that your needs will be met, giving you a greater ability to enjoy the material world.

The imprints from early family wounds are subconsciously stored in your first chakra, as well as beliefs from early conditioning that have become so ingrained, they are now instinctual. The energetic imprints from ancestors, along with past-life karma, are also subconsciously stored in your root chakra and need to be brought to light. Look to your first chakra for most of the insidious and ingrained patterns that obscure reality and pull you out of the flow.

Your first chakra is at the base of your spine and also rules your feet. It provides a base of support for healthy posture. Elimination is also a key function of your first chakra and is essential for good health of your body and psyche.

If you have a diminished first chakra, symptoms can include excessive fear over security, feelings of not belonging, and being ungrounded and flighty, with a generally weak physical constitution. There can be difficulty letting go of anything and elimination problems, as well as feet, lower back, and weight issues. Balancing these issues will be discussed in the "First Chakra Difficulties and Solutions" section later in this chapter.

Body Consciousness

Physical intelligence is an attribute of your first chakra and is revealed in how you care for your body and listen to its instincts not just to survive, but to thrive. Although the general requirements for all physical bodies to survive are the same, including adequate food, water, air, clothing, and shelter, each of us is in a unique physical body, with its own specific requirements to stay healthy and vital.

The same principle applies to the different varieties of vegetables and flowers in a garden. Generally, all plants need soil, water, and sun, but each plant has specific soil, water, and sunlight needs to thrive. It is the same with your unique body, and it is essential to know your body's specific diet, exercise, and environmental needs to thrive.

Perhaps you were raised on a healthy vegetarian diet that worked well for other members of your family, but you discovered that without meat and fish in your diet, you felt lethargic and sickly. The inverse of this could just as easily be the case. You must discover what is right for you and know what your needs are for a healthy diet. You must also know what environment and climate your body thrives in.

Your Fitness Rituals

Your fitness rituals are your day-to-day practices for keeping your body fit. Young people are typically healthy and fit, but when you see people who are healthy and fit from mid-life on, you know their personal rituals include a strong fitness regime. As we age, keeping the body tuned up becomes more of a necessity, and some training with strength, movement, posture, and flexibility is required if we are to be supported in our body and not dragged down by it.

If you don't know how to take care of your body, over time this neglect will lead to a body that is in the way of your well-being. It is hard to experience the incredible lightness of being when your body is dragging you down.

Posture

Your root chakra is the base that supports your entire system. It governs your feet and sitting bones, both of which are essential for healthy posture. Gravity is always working with you or against you, depending on your posture. You are sitting, walking, lifting, and standing all day long, with either good posture or poor posture, and the effects accumulate over time.

Exercise
. . . .
Regaining Posture While Sitting

Your sitting bones, the ischial bones of the pelvis, are the two bony protrusions on the underside of your seat that you can feel when sitting on a hard surface and rocking your pelvis forward and backward. When you are sitting for long periods of time, it is helpful to make minor adjustments so you can feel both sitting bones equally. Push into your sitting bones against your chair, and lift your rib cage and torso up from this grounded base.

Exercise
. . . .
Standing Posture for
Balance and Grounding

While standing, see if you can feel all four corners of your feet (the outer and inner corners of your heels and the balls of your feet) firmly on the ground. Push down into the ground and simultaneously lift your body up as if you were suspended by a cord above the crown of your head, pulling you upward. Push down and pull up simultaneously.
. . . .

Place and Belonging

Finding the right place for you to feel rooted is of primary importance with your first chakra. The environment that your Personal

Self thrives in is highly specific to each individual. Preferably, you would walk out the door from where you live and the climate, vegetation, and energetic feel for the land itself would feel vital to you. Ideally, your dwelling place would be a sanctuary for what nurtures and sustains your individual being when you just drop down into the place within yourself that is most at ease.

Along with where you belong, your belongings and personal possessions are also born of first chakra needs. Possessions substantiate a person's physical presence, and with some people this can get excessive. The ideal balance is having adequate resources to meet your needs comfortably but not so much that the managing and acquiring of those possessions occupies a disproportionate amount of your time, squeezing out time for other aspects of life.

Survival: What Are You Willing to Risk Life and Limb For?

The survival theme of the first chakra extends to those you are willing to risk life and limb for. This is the range of your first chakra and extends to family members you willingly provide for and protect. Environmentalists extend their first chakra's range to the needs of the planet for sustaining life. Crisis relief crews in disaster zones extend their first chakra to the needs of those in desperate peril.

Emergency and social workers of all types, healers, and therapists working for the survival needs of others in times of crisis are working with the survivor archetype not within themselves but for people, plants, and animals who actually are in a survival situation. EMTs, firefighters, police officers, emergency room nurses, avalanche ski patrol volunteers, military personnel, and people who protect pets and ensure their survival are other examples of those extending their first chakra's reach to include others.

Security

Feeling safe and secure is another primary need of your first chakra. Having adequate resources to cover the basic needs of life—food, clothing, shelter, communication, and transportation—is essential to avoid triggering the alarm of your security chakra. Having an abundance of resources would be even better, with the possessions we acquire reinforcing our first chakra and our physical footprint on the earth.

A key principle in understanding how to bring your first chakra's needs into balance is to be aware of the insatiable nature of all your lower chakras if you are only looking externally for fulfillment. All three lower chakras can be brought into a sense of fullness only when integrated within the system of your other chakras. If you are looking for fulfillment in life only through your money and possessions, there will never be enough to satisfy the sense of incompleteness you feel. As you awaken to the higher chakras and the expanded world of experience that opens before you, you simply choose to disengage from identifying yourself exclusively with the limited range of the lower chakras' experiences in life, having found greater treasures elsewhere.

As you awaken to your Higher Self through your upper chakras, security issues start falling away and you begin to work with the world rather than against it. When you follow your true nature revealed through your Higher Self, life works because it is in its nature to do so. It takes a bit of faith to trust that your

Higher Self is aligned with the greater web of existence, the Tao of creation, which will have no difficulty providing for your needs. You are part of the same fabric and are sustained by the same force as all of nature. A tree doesn't have to work at becoming a tree; it is in its nature to do so. So it is with your true nature—you do not have to work at becoming your true nature; it is already within you.

This manifesting power of aligning with your true nature is described as *Te* in the teachings of the *Tao Te Ching* and is expressed in this passage from Chuang-Tzu's delightful commentaries on Taoism from the third century BCE:

> When a man has perfect virtue [is aligned with one's true nature, *Te*], fire cannot burn him, water cannot drown him, cold and heat cannot afflict him, birds and beasts cannot injure him. [1]

This shows how living aligned with your Higher Self is a powerful security policy for your first chakra. If you were in touch with your Higher Self while grounded and centered in your body and a tree branch was about to fall right where you were sitting, just before it happened you would be led to get up and move— maybe to get a drink of water or to make a call—but one way or another you would be led to move out of harm's way.

This teaching substantiates faith that living aligned with your true nature will provide for all your first chakra security needs, even abundantly so. When you are in touch with your true na-

---

1. Chuang-Tzu, *The Complete Chuang Tzu*, trans. Burton Watson (New York: Columbia University Press, 1968), p. 182.

ture and are in harmony with life, you are aligned with both your individual Te and the Tao of existence. Aligning with the Tao brings the benefit of increased tranquility in your life, but it also has built-in safety measures. Since all of life is interconnected, if danger is approaching from any direction, the Tao will lead you to safety, even before the threat arrives.

Another way to picture how your security is interconnected within a greater system is to imagine that you are a cell in your body. How can you, as an individual cell, feel secure that your needs will be met? You would not need to learn how to fulfill your role; a cell would naturally do so. Since it is in the body's best interest that the cell fulfill its function, the body will naturally provide for all the cell's needs. The cell would not become more secure by defending itself against the rest of the body; in fact, the exact opposite is true. The cell doesn't even need to know that it needs oxygen, blood, and nutrients. The body knows this and automatically supplies all of these things. If the cell is in alignment with the needs of the body, all of its individual needs will be met.

Trust that it is in your best interest for your security needs to form a symbiotic relationship with the life force around you. Trust that if you do your part to tend to the responsibilities that have been assigned to you, it is in the Tao's best interest to care for all of your needs.

Practice
. . . .
Affirmations for Feeling Secure

• *I am thankful for my body today and the gift it has given me for experiencing life on earth.*

- *I am safe and secure and know that my life force will rise to meet all that life brings to me today.*
- *I am a creature of the earth and I belong here. I claim my space.*
- *I am centered and grounded in my body and am ready to take on all that life brings to me today.*

Subconscious Motivations

Your first chakra encompasses your subconscious—the storehouse of buried fears, imprints from early family life concerning security, and even past-life karma. Identifying buried subconscious material is particularly difficult because by definition you are not conscious of it. You can't see subconscious material directly anymore than you can see the wind directly. You see the trees sway and the leaves blow and you know that it is windy. You don't look for the wind; you look for its effects by observing its impact on the environment. Such is the case with your subconscious—you can't see it directly, but you can get to know it by its impact.

Reoccurring anxiety concerning security when nothing in your life warrants this panic is like leaves blowing in the wind. Consider your mother's issues with security while you were in the womb, at the time of your birth, and during the first few years of your life. Was she perhaps anxious about security and safety, leaving an energetic imprint in your energy field before you were even conscious? These energetic imprints can be identified and made conscious. When you are conscious of the source of your experience of anxiety, you can work with it when it arises.

Excessive attachment to family background, beliefs, and superstitions rooted in your first chakra can hold you back from discovering your own authentic truth. As you awaken to your upper chakras, your interest in truth outweighs these attachments and you begin to liberate yourself from inherited beliefs that do not resonate with your truth.

Past-Life Karma

Past-life karma is also stored in the subconscious region of your first chakra. Most simply said, karma is the fruits of your actions, for good or ill, and ultimately we are responsible for all of our actions, whether in previous lives, this life, or the next. Past-life karma comes from unresolved issues from your previous lives that is coming to light again in this life, weaving themes from your soul's journey in previous incarnations into the script of your current life. Karmic patterns stemming from the unconscious continue to exist until they are brought into conscious awareness. With conscious awareness of what was once unconscious, you harvest the "aha" moment of understanding the lesson, allowing you to move forward in life with wisdom rather than karmic seeds.

Even the good karma from previous lives can skew a person's compass in this life. I've worked with many clients over the years who resonate with the karma of a devout seeker in their previous lives and are having inexplicable difficulty finding healthy relationships and prosperity in this life. Whether the devout past life was rooted in a yogic or a religious tradition, taking a solemn vow of poverty, chastity, and obedience as the way to God could have very easily been part of the path.

Now in this life, something always seems to sabotage the person's efforts to find a healthy sexual relationship or a prosperous career. It could be that vows made in earnest before God can never be broken, even from life to life. Although the vows can't be broken, they can be amended and broadened to acknowledge the presence of the divine in this life while maintaining healthy relationships and experiencing prosperity.

With awakening, you have an opportunity to liberate yourself from the underlying karmic patterns that manifest as continually acting out unconscious behavior patterns in certain areas of life. You can be practicing mindful awareness in most areas of your life, but with certain habits or patterns, it is as if you go momentarily unconscious and act without conscious consideration. For example, an obsession with sex can manifest even for an awakened person as kundalini heats up karmic seeds and brings them to life and awakens the *possibility* to become conscious of what you weren't conscious of before.

Destructive habits that you unconsciously rationalize in the moment because you need them just to get by (survive) can be traced to karmic seeds stored in your first chakra. Whether these seeds are from early childhood, past-life karma, or painful, repressed memories in this life, they hijack your ability to use your free will consciously, distorting your awareness with subconscious motivations. You can't see reality clearly as long as your vision is skewed by these early imprints.

The key to breaking free of this tendency of justifying going unconscious after identifying the pattern is to not go unconscious! If the problem is going unconscious, then stay conscious, not just after your consciousness comes back and you feel remorseful for your behavior but also in the moment. Stay consciously aware of the fact that you are going unconscious; watch for the moment when the justifications and rationalizations begin—that is the moment. Catch it there and choose to stay consciously aware of it, and unconscious patterns will dissipate.

Say you are trying to quit a bad habit, such as smoking or a sugar addiction, and have failed many times in the past. Consciously you know it is in your best interest to quit, yet something always sabotages your efforts. If you catch the moment when you first start making justifications for your unconscious behavior, it will greatly facilitate your efforts. We are calling smoking or indulging in sweets unconscious behavior in this example because consciously you have already made the decision to quit. What voice were you listening to when the justifications began? A rationalization for going against what you consciously know is in your best interest always comes from the ego and the Lower Self. Don't just fight the urge; fight the rationalizations and justifications that erode conscious awareness.

First Chakra for the Spiritually Inclined

For those of a spiritual nature, the first chakra issues of security and materialism may seem far removed; but while in a body, you still have a first chakra, and it is important to keep it vital and healthy. When you honor your body as the gift creation has given to you to experience this incarnation, you honor both your body and your spiritual nature.

To include your first chakra in your spiritual life, realize the importance of a regular practice to develop strong spiritual "roots." A spiritual practice is engaging regularly in activities that feed your spirit. It could be formal, such as a regular yoga routine, meditation practice, or attending Catholic Mass, or informal, such as a morning walk honoring the sunrise and the birth of the new day, reading sacred literature and poetry, or listening to recordings of speakers who feed your soul.

This battle to live a life guided by your Higher Self must be won each and every day, and having a regular spiritual practice of one type or another gives you the security of knowing it will always be there when you return to it.

For the spiritually inclined, a healthy first chakra can be seen in the principles you stand on as the basis of your personal being, such as *ahimsa*, the principle of nonviolence toward all living things. Perhaps the principle of nonviolence is not just a belief for you but is a baseline principle that guides your life—but where do you draw the line with this principle? Where can you draw the line?

I'm a vegetarian and I try to adhere to the principle of ahimsa as best I can. I love to grow a vegetable garden, and every spring, when I clear the garden of the weeds and grasses that have taken root there since last season, I'm confronted with where to draw the line on the principle of ahimsa. In the moment, my clearing of the weeds is such a violent act to the plants that have already established this as their home. I realize there is only so far I can go with ahimsa and still honor my own need to survive. I do the best I can to honor the sacrifice these weeds are making for the garden and acknowledge their role in making the compost that will, in turn, feed the soil.

And so it is with your first chakra: you have to claim your right to exist, because if you don't, nature will swallow up your footprints. While you're here on earth, you have to claim your space and, in a sense, fight back against nature's attempts to undo your efforts. Hiring someone else to spray for bugs, setting traps and bait for rodent control, and applying wood preservative to extinguish possible mold growth are all examples of how the first chakra's need to survive can test the limits of loftier principles.

First Chakra
Difficulties and Solutions

First chakra blocks can manifest as security issues, hoarding, a lack of groundedness, attachment to family conditioning, primal ancestral fears, and past-life karmic issues. We will explore these potential difficulties as well as methods for restoring balance.

Security Issues

The psychological need to feel safe and secure is a primal drive of your first chakra and is not easy to experience in a culture that encourages a philosophy of "more is better." In a capitalist system, experiencing security is not encouraged; pursuing it is, but not experiencing it. No matter how much you have, you could always have a bit more, just in case. That is a side effect of capitalism. It's not good or bad; it just is. If we felt secure and had all we needed, who would turn the wheels of commerce? You have to break free of the cultural neurosis about security in order to feel secure.

In a debt-based economy such as ours, it is easy to feel insecure about mounting debt that you may acquire to make it in our economic system. This vulnerability to insecurity is especially strong when a person is just starting out at building a life and looks at the debt from education loans, mortgages, and the like. The cultural neurosis over debt stems from believing that security will come from having all that debt paid off, making the need of the first chakra to feel secure unattainable today in the present moment.

Exercise
. . . .

Experiencing Security
While Paying Bills

At bill-paying time of the month, when money might be a little tight and while looking at all the daunting numbers in front of me, those familiar feelings of insecurity often grab my attention, tightening my energy field with fear. In times like these, I like to go out of doors to shake off those feelings and simply contemplate the inexhaustible life force I see all around me in nature. It animates the plants without any effort, as well as the birds, the trees, the grass, and the bugs, all vibrant with this inexhaustible life force coursing through their being.

It doesn't take but a few minutes of contemplation for me to realize that this same life force is moving through me, animating my being. This wonderful realization that life is living me as much as I am living life washes over me, and feelings of insecurity vanish as I feel this deep connection. When I go back to paying the bills, I am no longer pulled into the cultural neurosis over debt, and I get on with the process of managing my debts from a place of security within me—taking an inside-out approach.

. . . .

Hoarding

There are two different types of hoarding that stem from an imbalanced first chakra. The first type of hoarding is when you have more than you realistically need and can use yet you still are acquiring more. This type of over-acquiring of possessions is quite common in a materialistic culture that encourages this behavior, and again, you have to be able to compensate for the background cultural messages that promote this excessiveness to find your own right balance.

The second type of hoarding comes from a deficiency in the first chakra's role in elimination. In the body, this can manifest as constipation as well as issues involving the colon and large intestine. In terms of behavior, this can manifest as not letting go of possessions even when they have no value or purpose. In extreme examples, you can hardly walk through the house for all the piled junk in the way. This failure to release possessions clogs the system right at the base. Excessively holding on to possessions blocks the flow of more coming into your life.

My wife is excellent at this elimination role of the first chakra. She has a "pass it on" area on our back porch that she is constantly adding to with all the stuff that accumulates past its value. She then distributes this out into the community, where it can be put to use. We have a large family, and it always amazes me how much stuff comes in the door to support us. I'm thankful Laurie is just as good at making sure that as much stuff goes out the back door.

Practice
. . . .
Prime the Abundance Pump
by Giving

At times when you feel stuck financially or are wrestling with insecurity, prime the abundance pump by practicing generosity. Donate to charity, give something you value to someone who needs it, or tip a little more when the service warrants it. These and other acts of generosity will open a closed first chakra. To help keep your security chakra open, you could use this affirmation as you are writing checks: *Joyously I give and joyously I receive.*

. . . .

Lack of Groundedness

A diminished first chakra often manifests as a lack of groundedness, leading to chaos and a life out of control. When you are barely in your body and everything seems like it is too much to handle, you are experiencing a lack of groundedness. A clue would be the saying "I just can't survive another day like this." The first advice in times like these is to get back in your body!

Exercise

. . . .

Grounding Yourself When Anxious

Breathe deep into your body and notice your feet firmly on the floor. Sit tall and erect and push your root chakra firmly into your chair while pulling the rest of your spine upward. Focus on your breath and posture to bring you back to the present moment.

Go for a walk in nature and force yourself to pay attention to every step and maintain an acute awareness of only the sights and sounds arising in the moment. The sound of your breath, the sensation of each foot touching the earth, the sound of a bird, the rustle of the wind, and the sensations arising from your skin all can bring you into the present moment, where grounding occurs.

. . . .

Primal Fears

Primal fears, such as the fear of snakes, are encoded in your first chakra and serve a healthy function in survival. Experiences of shock trauma from traumatic events leading to PTSD (post-traumatic stress disorder) are stored deep in the subconscious memory of the first chakra and obviously do not serve a healthy function.

Rolfing and other forms of deep tissue massage can often help bring to the surface these subconsciously held memories stored in deep muscle cellular memory, to begin the healing of experiences of shock trauma. Meditation and mindfulness training are particularly helpful in releasing these buried and stuck energies. You can learn to stay in mindful awareness when a panic attack arises, and then instead of resisting it, pushing it away, or backing down, you can simply let it be without acting on it. Staying anchored in the Observer of your Higher Self, you notice the panic rising, feel its energetic effects, and watch it pass. If you stay consistent with this practice each and every time a feeling of panic arises, it will begin to lose its energetic punch, eventually becoming a memory moving before your inner eye without its energetic wallop.

Body Pain

Pain in the body from illness or injury can dominate your awareness of your first chakra. As the body ages, aches and pains seem to come with the territory, and when talking to people who are elderly, who are all too painfully aware of this phenomenon, it often occupies their consciousness and conversation. We know it is hard to be joyful when our body is in pain, and yet does this mean that aging will lead to a lack of joy?

The Buddha gave some guidance in this regard when, legend has it, he and some of his followers were on a journey to the next village and the weather turned foul and quite cold. His followers were complaining among themselves about the dreadful conditions and noticed that the Buddha seemed unruffled despite the dire circumstances. When they questioned him as to how he could remain unbothered by the weather, his response was, "I am just Buddha experiencing cold—I'm still Buddha." The Buddha's self-identity was anchored in the ultimate expression of the Higher Self, aware of the body but not the body.

Activities to Empower Your First Chakra

The first chakra is of the earth element, and getting out into raw nature always revitalizes the primal nature of your root chakra. The wilder and more untouched the nature, the better. Participating directly in hunter-gatherer activities, such as cultivating a vegetable garden, fishing, hunting, or raising livestock for food, directly benefits your root chakra. Gathering wild mushrooms and berries or gathering and chopping firewood are other examples of activities that feed your survival chakra. In the city, you could closely observe the behavior of wild birds in a tree or stop to admire the tenacity of life evidenced in a plant growing in a crack in the sidewalk to help connect you to your primal nature.

Fitness training of all types is the most direct method of activating your first chakra. Hiking and even walking, as simple as these activities are, are some of the best ways to keep your first chakra healthy. For other people, it is time spent at the gym or involvement with sports that empowers their first chakra.

As you develop your first chakra awareness, you begin to notice even the slightest nuances of energy sensations manifesting in your body, from the dense vibration of physical pain to the subtle awareness of where you are holding needless tension in your body.

Exercise
. . . .

Do an Energy Check
on Your Body Periodically

Periodically throughout the day, it is a good practice to sit still for a moment with your spine straight and, after a few deep breaths, scan your body from head to feet and notice where you are holding tension. Breathe deep into the tight area of your body and consciously release the tension. Is it in your shoulders? You don't need your shoulders tensed to sit. Let go of the tension and breathe a sense of calm and ease into your body. Is the tension in your solar plexus? Breathe deeply and let it go.

. . . .

Additional Activities
to Enhance Your First Chakra

Yoga Postures

Yoga postures that are particularly beneficial for your root chakra are squatting pose, knees-to-chest pose, bridge pose, pelvic tilts, mountain pose, and all standing poses.

First Chakra Breathing

Tighten the sphincter muscle between the anus and the genitals while breathing deep into the base of your spine. On the out-breath, relax the root lock while toning the seed sound for the first chakra: *Lam* (rhymes with "mom"). Picture the color red radiating from your first chakra as you breathe.

Astrocartography

An astrocartography map shows where each of the planets in your astrological birth chart will have their strongest influence on the entire earth. Having your astrocartography read by an astrologer can give you good clues to where on the planet you could feel energetically at your best.

Body Associations

The spine, legs, feet, bones, teeth, prostate, bladder, blood, tailbone, elimination system, and sense of smell are all associated with the first chakra. Difficulties in any of these areas of the body show a need to bring this chakra into balance.

First Chakra Foods

Root vegetables, protein-rich foods, and red foods enhance your first chakra. Potatoes, beets, radishes, parsnips, carrots, turnips, mushrooms, eggs, butter, fish, lean meats, beans, tofu, soy, nut butters, pomegranates, strawberries, raspberries, tomatoes, cayenne, and paprika all stimulate your first chakra.

First Chakra Gemstones and Crystals

Ruby, garnet, hematite, obsidian, smoky quartz, black tourmaline, jasper, onyx, bloodstone, and plain rocks all benefit your first chakra. These can be especially helpful at times when you need to ground and restore strength to your physical body.

Crystals and gemstones can be used to help amplify a chakra when it is sluggish and can aid in healing a chakra when needed. To amplify a chakra, you can carry a particular stone or crystal in your pocket or place it on your desk or workspace. For healing work, placing the crystal directly on the chakra or its associated parts of the body while lying on your back will enhance its impact even more.

First Chakra Journaling

Before moving on to your second chakra, it can be helpful to record your insights and things you want to remember about your first chakra in your journal. How do you see it operating in your life? You will likely receive guidance and nudges from your Higher Self on what you can do to enhance your first chakra.

List the pluses and minuses of your experiences with your first chakra. Where is it that you could improve and strengthen your root chakra, and what activities and exercises could help you do this? What aspects of your first chakra do you already feel good about and have direct experience in knowing how it is operating in your life? Did you receive insights into where subconscious motivations have been hampering the balance of your first chakra? Recording your insights in your journal will help you maintain conscious awareness of where you need to liberate yourself from these subconscious behavior patterns to restore health to your root chakra.

. . . .

CHAPTER 3

Second Chakra: Svadhisthana

Location: Just above the pubic bone

Element: Water

Symbol: An upturned crescent moon within a circle with six lotus petals

Color: Orange

Principles: Duality and cyclic change, emotions

Key Benefit: Experiencing the joy of the senses

Key Obstacles: Guilt, attachment/aversions, and denial of emotions

Spiritual Quality: Seeing beauty as a spiritual doorway

Type of Intelligence: Emotional

Your second chakra is of the water element and gives you the capacity to feel and adapt to the constant ebb and flow of your emotions and the cyclic nature of reality. This chakra is lunar, feminine, and yin in nature and is your wellspring for emotional, creative, sensual, and sexual energies. This is where you experience passion and enthusiasm for life and derive much enjoyment from the sensory world. Beyond just surviving, your second chakra awakens your ability to enjoy the delights of the senses available from being in a body.

When your second chakra is balanced and open, you have abundant enthusiasm for life and are able to be present with the full range of emotions that arise in intimate relationships without being overwhelmed by them. You are able to enjoy the beauty of nature, music, art, and the aesthetics of life, and you likely have a creative outlet that allows you to pour your abundant feelings into some form of creative expression. You enjoy the warmth of intimacy and affection from relationships in your life without being dominated by your sexuality.

When your second chakra is repressed, blocked, or inhibited, the sweetness of life is missed. You can become bitter without the ability to enjoy life. Emotions are troublesome or denied when your second chakra is diminished, and you can have difficulty adapting to change. Balancing these issues will be discussed in the "Second Chakra Difficulties and Solutions" section later in this chapter.

Pleasure Seeking

Svadhisthana is the Sanskrit name for the second chakra and translates as "one's abode" as well as "to taste with pleasure and to seek delight." Regardless of how refined your tastes are, pleasure seeking in one form or another is the second chakra's orientation to life. Once the survival and security needs of your first chakra are met, your second chakra's attachment to pleasure is one of the strongest and most alluring pulls of your Personal Self. The delight and fascination with the senses and their magnetic pull can never be satiated, as the sensory world will always entice you with its kaleidoscopic, ever-changing fascinations. For a spiritually inclined individual, or even a person who wants some productivity in life, this gravitational pull has to be brought into control to get anything done, or to become aware of parts of one's character beyond the second chakra's range of pleasure seeking.

Passion, in both its healthy and unhealthy manifestations, springs from your second chakra. Your pleasure chakra is also linked to the unconscious, and it fuels drives, desires, and attachments lurking beneath the surface of conscious awareness. Unacknowledged desires and unresolved emotional wounds get pushed beneath the surface of conscious awareness and skew one's emotional compass.

When unconscious passions are given license, they are rarely healthy and are most often destructive; but when passion comes from fully surrendering to an experience in the moment, whether it is love's embrace or a creative project that you feel passionate about, this is the sweet kiss of an awakened and balanced second chakra. When your pleasure seeking is directed toward memory or the future, this is unfilled desire. When pleasure is found in the immediate here and now, this is passionate delight!

Your second chakra is also the storehouse of *samskaras*, the karmic seeds from past desires and charged emotional energy. This seedbed of potential karma lies dormant in your subconscious until, like seeds in the ground when given a little water, they spring into life. This makes the second chakra one of the most complicated of all the chakras because of all the compelling attractions in life constantly tempting these buried samskaras.

Contemplation

. . . .

Where Might Unwanted Desires Be Leftover Karma?

It can be helpful to contemplate where unwanted desires (such as an attraction to a married co-worker) that distract and even torment your psyche might possibly be leftover karma. Looking at the desire as your karma, you know it will continue to show up in your life until you bring it into conscious awareness by naming the desire as it arises and knowing that it is fool's gold it is offering.

. . . .

The Fluid Movement of Emotions

The symbol of the crescent moon reveals the cyclic and ever-changing lunar nature of your second chakra. Each month the moon goes through its complete cycle, from new moon to full moon and back again. The moon's effect on the element of water is evidenced by the tides of the great oceans moving from high tide to low tide in rhythmic measure. To go with the flow of your second chakra requires you to align with the tides of your emotions rather than resist them.

In a culture that doesn't understand the natural tidal nature of emotions, this cyclic nature of one's emotions is seen as problematic, with emotions being thought of as up or down, good or bad. Shifting your attitude from *up* and *down* to *outward* and *inward* changes things altogether. Up and down imply that something is right or wrong about your emotions; outward and inward remove the stigma and encourage you to explore the inward-turning tide of your emotional cycle in healthy ways, such as by reading certain books, listening to music, spending quality alone time in nature, or engaging in spiritual activities such as meditation, all of which are introspective and healthy.

The cycle of rain is also a good representation of the fluid, flowing, and transformative nature of the element of water and emotions. Water is released from the clouds as rain and becomes absorbed into the soil, then is drawn up by roots into plants and ultimately is released back into the atmosphere. Similarly, emotions are absorbed by the subconscious, arise into your conscious awareness, and are then released back into the atmosphere in whatever way you give them expression.

It is important to keep the cycle moving by feeling emotions as they arise into your conscious awareness and then are released. When you repress, block, or deny your emotions, the cycle is interrupted and problems begin to manifest in your health and relationships.

If you don't understand this cyclic nature of your second chakra, you might fight the natural cycle and "feel" (key to the second chakra) distraught over the low phase. Only wanting the highs and not the lows leads to the phenomenon of changing a shirt to fix a bad back. You might think to yourself, "If I don't always feel the same high I once did with my partner, it must be her. I'll get rid of her and attract someone into my life who is always up, on, and ready." Good luck with that, right?

Addictions of all sorts are fueled by this lack of ability to align with the lunar, cyclic nature of the second chakra. Food and shopping addictions stem from an attempt to always feel good, up, and happy by filling the void of emptiness one might associate with the inward-turning, low-tide phase.

Attempting to avoid all sadness and experience only joy is like trying to keep a pendulum only on the up phase of its arc by blocking its retreating movement. By blocking the sadness, you also inhibit the joy.

Second chakra emotions are soft, watery emotions that evoke tears of joy and sadness like a good tearjerker movie or book does. A person with an open second chakra is passionate in their feelings—sad when feeling sad is appropriate and glad when feeling glad is appropriate.

Empathy is the ability to feel within yourself the emotions of others and is born from an awakened second chakra. It can be very confusing if you are awakening to increased empathy without knowing that is what is going on. Imagine carrying someone else's emotions within you unknowingly and trying to understand why you feel the way you do when the source of the emotions is not within you. On days when you feel emotionally muddled and can't get a handle on why you feel the way you do, consider that you might be opening up empathetically and trying to process the emotions of others as if they were your own.

Practice
· ·

Feel It, Bless It, Release It

When you are feeling emotionally confused, it can be helpful to try the practice of "feel it, bless it, release it" just for a few minutes, and you will be amazed at how often you pull up out of the emotional muddle and realize it wasn't your experience you were trying to process.

Notice the conspicuous absence of the words "analyze it" in this exercise. You have already tried analyzing your emotional state in an attempt to track its source to no avail, so you specifically let go of trying to figure out this emotional energy you are experiencing.

With "feel it," allow yourself to simply feel the nature of the emotional state you are experiencing without wishing it were in any way different. What is its flavor, its tone? It helps to imagine how many people in the world must be feeling just such an emotion at this time. If the feeling is insecurity for no apparent reason, feel it and imagine how many homeless, jobless, hopeless people in the world must be feeling this very emotion at this moment. Don't hide or color the emotional state; just be with it.

With "bless it," picture pulling the feeling of the emotion right into your lower belly at your second chakra, and then, on your inbreath, picture pulling the energy up through your chakras, purifying the emotional energy as it moves up through your compassionate heart.

With "release it," you can picture the energy moving up and out through your upper chakras. You could lay these emotions on the lap of God, or you could simply release the energy through your crown chakra with your own silent prayer that all beings be free of suffering.

Do this cycle several times, at least for a few minutes, and most often you will rise up out of the muddle. You will still be aware of the emotion in the background, but not identifying the source of the emotion as within you will free your psyche from its confusion. On the occasions when this practice doesn't work to release you from the emotional grip of an emotion, the source of the emotion is most likely your own personal issue and needs to be dealt with as such. But at least you will know that.

Imagine being a creature of the water realm, such as a fish. A fish wouldn't be able to say "I'm not going to get wet today" any more than one could choose not to feel emotions at the second chakra. Also, the fish wouldn't be able to identify the source of any drop of water that it feels any more than the mind can identify the reason for many of the feelings and emotions arising from the second chakra.

. . . .

Duality, Polarity, Taste, and Projection

Your second chakra is where your likes and dislikes register— what you enjoy and therefore what you don't enjoy. Linked to the unconscious, many of your attractions and dislikes arise subconsciously and get projected onto the world. The measure of knowing whether your behavior is being animated by the healthy likes and dislikes of your personal tastes or is coming from unconsciously skewed reactions to life is in the strength of your reaction. Unclaimed aspects of your psyche get pushed down in the subconscious and then get projected onto others. This process of *projection* has to be understood to liberate the unconscious energy.

Likes and dislikes fall in the range of your preferences and natural tastes. Projections, on the other hand, are parts of your character that have been rejected by your conscious awareness and get projected onto others.

The difference between taste and projection is in the strength of the response. If you walk into a restaurant and notice people talking loudly in one area of the restaurant and, preferring a quieter atmosphere, choose a table away from the noisy ones and go about enjoying your evening, this is your preference. If, on the other hand, you find their behavior so upsetting that you can't even enjoy your meal, then it is likely a projection.

Become aware of the things about others that you dislike the most. What personality traits in others trigger a gut reaction—more than simply not liking the behavior but a strong reaction? That which we deny within ourselves gets projected onto others. When you are in the presence of this type of behavior, ask yourself, "How much energy is going into my resistance, what is my resistance protecting, and why?" There is probably a great deal of obnoxious behavior in the world that you overlook, so why is this particular behavior able to throw you for a loop?

That which we push away from us hardens, freezes, lingers, and cannot change. Whatever we deny about ourselves and have a gut-level aversion to owns us as much as attachments to pleasure do. The parts of you that you just don't like about yourself are the very qualities that persist and harden and, in that state, can't change.

The qualities we most dislike about our parents often get pushed down in the psyche and are a common source of rejected and then projected emotions. How often we hear, "I can't believe I'm acting just like my mother!"

The antidote is to allow the feelings, stay in conscious awareness of their source, and feel the emotional wave move through your body without attempting to fix it or change it. Let it wash over you and subside on its own.

Magnetism, Values, and Your Second Chakra

A balanced and open second chakra enhances your magnetism. As you allow more of the joy and delight of life into your emotional field, your magnetic nature is enhanced, attracting more of life to you. Without strong personal values governing what you accept from all that you attract to you, your life would devolve into hedonism and a house of cards. Just because you attract something to you doesn't mean it is always in your best interest!

Your second chakra doesn't have willpower by itself. Willpower awakens with your third chakra, so what will stop your second chakra from constant pleasure seeking? Your values—such as fidelity, honesty, a healthy body, a loving family, and a healthy planet. These values, more than willpower, are what channel your magnetism into what is healthy for you.

Feeling unattractive can also arise in your second chakra when it is not open. Although we all can't look like movie stars, we all have a second chakra and the magnetism that comes from fully enjoying life. When you are feeling insecure about your attractiveness, your energy field becomes constricted and tarnished by your negative feelings about yourself and you become less magnetic and less attractive—yikes! The solution is to spend more time focusing on what you enjoy, are attracted to, and find beautiful. This fills your energy field with beauty, and being full of beauty is beautiful. This sends out a magnetic signal of what you actually enjoy rather than what you are dissatisfied with, and attracts people who are drawn to your magnetic enjoyment of life.

We all know people who are not perfect in their looks, but their love of life and their enjoyment of your company make them beautiful in your eyes and very attractive. Is it their clothes, hairstyle, jewelry, or body type that makes them attractive? Likely not. More likely it is their energy itself that is captivating.

Practice
. . . .
Learning to Enjoy Your Way to an Enjoyable Life

Your natural magnetic energy can be enhanced by entering into an appreciation of the enjoyable moments in life that do show up, not by reaching, grasping, building, wishing, or longing for enjoyment that isn't there in the moment. Learn to magnetize the enjoyable moments by entering into an appreciation of the experiences. Learn to linger in the enjoyment of life's delightful moments, from simple pleasures to rare special moments. Lingering in the appreciation of these enjoyable moments sends out a magnetic signal of enjoyment, attracting to you more of that which you enjoy with gratitude.
. . . .

Affection to Sexuality to Intimacy

From the sensuality of simple affection to the sexuality of intimacy, your second chakra's need for touch is one of its main drives. The skin cells of your body are fed by healthy touch and affection as much as your stomach is fed by food. Children who grow up touch-starved are not as "comfortable in their own skin" as those who grow up in affectionate families. If this was your experience growing up, it can help to get plenty of healthy massages to feed those long-hungry skin cells. In relationships, cultivating affection that doesn't always lead to greater sport is a great way to soothe and comfort the body. Warm baths, hot tubs, and indulgent showers nurture those hungry skin cells as well.

The survival of the species requires procreation for new children to be born and is a primal drive of your first chakra. Sex simply for the pure enjoyment of the experience is of the second chakra. All species of animals must procreate, but only humans, dolphins, and bonobos are known to enjoy their sexuality outside of procreation. This rare ability to enjoy one of the primal drives for the pure pleasure of the experience sounds so natural and delightful yet can be quite confusing, as each person must find their own way in the labyrinth of human sexuality.

Disappointments that come from unmet needs and desires are agonizing and are a common cause of discontent in relationships. Before you go too far into the disappointment, first ask yourself if you have revealed your desires to your partner. Assuming that others should know what is hidden in you creates unnecessary torment. Although revealing your unseen needs is important in all meaningful relationships, it is particularly important in intimate relationships.

If you are experiencing the disappointment of your desires and needs not being met in your relationship, first look to see if you have revealed your hidden desires to your partner. Have you fallen into the trap of expecting your partner to be nearly psychic, thinking, "If he really loved me, he would know my needs and desires. I shouldn't have to tell him if he really cared." This type of thinking invariably leads to disappointment. To experience intimacy beyond sex, you must be willing to reveal to your partner what pleases you—not by handing your partner a script of how to please you, but by gently guiding your lover to your sweetness. Be willing to share your treasures.

For those in an ongoing relationship, gentle communication is required to work with getting your needs met while honoring the sexual self-esteem of your partner. This continues to be important as a relationship matures through the years. Enjoyment of sexuality and intimacy can continue late into life but requires periodic tune-up communication concerning the ever-changing and evolving needs and joys of each other's sexuality.

Creativity

The urge for creative self-expression can lead you to the arts or can manifest as something as simple as how you set a table and prepare a meal for the pure enjoyment of the experience. Being creative with how you arrange your house can transform it from being simply functional to being cozy, warm, and aesthetically appealing. Creativity is bringing beauty into a world that would otherwise be drab. Awakened second chakra energy is felt as arousal. When the lotus flower of your second chakra is pointed downward, it activates desire for sexual and sensory gratification, and when the lotus is pointed upward, the desire is for joyful creative expression.

The Artist Blues

After completing a major show, event, or performance that you've been working on for months or more, be prepared for the crash of the "artist blues." That which has occupied your thoughts, passions, hopes, and fears is now over, and you feel the resultant sadness that comes from a loss of identity. When last season's flower has faded after its moment in the sun, the cycle turns inward and a new seed is formed by taking the genetic best of the previous cycle. This inward turning—harvesting the wisdom and insights gained from the previous cycle while preparing for the next germination cycle—is necessary. Creative people understand the time it takes musing about, waiting for the next creative spark to catch fire.

Blocked Creativity

The second chakra's natural orientation leads to joyful creative expression of one type or another. Those who have stopped taking risks of creative expression in their life most likely have encountered some type of negative feedback concerning their creativity and have retreated to a safer path. "Your creative interests aren't going to lead you to a real job." "I don't think there would be a market for your idea." "You don't have the right kind of talent to be successful at that." This type of feedback from others is crippling to the natural creative expression of your second chakra.

Watching children at play can teach you the way to reclaim your freedom of creative expression. Observe how naturally creative children are at inventing games spontaneously, creating roads, houses, and forts out of anything available and then knocking down the creation they just built with a flying monster—and then starting all over again, the whole time laughing, bantering, and making up stories. Here we see the freedom of creative expression of an uninhibited second chakra.

Three important features of creative expression stand out: play, willingness to take creative risks, and non-attachment to the outcome.

The Creative Mindset

Whether it is in the arts, one's lifestyle, or one's career ambitions, creativity requires a different mindset than does productivity. Knowledge is helpful for being productive. The productive mindset of everyday life filters all the vast incoming information into that which serves the task you are trying to get done and accomplished. A productive mind is necessary to carry out the responsibilities of making our lives work. Everything is looked at in terms getting each task done efficiently. Risks and distractions are to be avoided so as to not waste time. The goal of the productive mindset is the outcome.

Creativity requires a different mindset. The creative mindset looks to see things outside of what is already known and thus adopts an entirely different attitude—a playful attitude willing to risk making mistakes. Creativity is often fueled by "happy mistakes" that weren't planned, and yet the mistake sometimes turns out better than what was planned. The productive mindset looks at a situation to find the most practical approach, whereas the creative mindset looks at a situation in terms of "what are the possibilities here?"

Creativity cannot be harnessed by the clock and show up on demand at 9:00 a.m. The muses show up when they show up, most often not when you plan for them. If you were to watch a creative artist at work in her studio, you would not see her being productive the entire time. There would be a considerable amount of time when the artist just seems to be musing, wandering around her studio, or staring vacantly out the window.

Creative insight is born in the quiet space between thoughts. The creative person is looking for inspiration beyond what they already know, and thus they need time for musing and getting out of the current track of thinking about the project at hand. A bit of this vacant musing creates the space for the flashes of fresh insight that come when they come.

Second Chakra
for the Spiritually Inclined

For those of a spiritual nature, beauty itself becomes a spiritual doorway and is readily found. Light reflecting off water, beautiful music and art, and the taste of something exquisite all become like spiritual experiences, bringing that same uplifting of the spirit and absorption into the moment. Making love changes from the goal of reaching the peak of orgasm to enjoying and lingering in all of the energetic stages you and your partner experience along the way. Having sex transforms into making love with your partner at the physical, emotional, mental, and spiritual levels after awakening to the spiritual qualities of sexuality.

Second Chakra
Difficulties and Solutions

When your second chakra is blocked or restricted, you can feel dull, a lack of joy, a lack of desire, or even depressed. A lack of sweetness in life leads to a bitter taste. Difficulty with your emotional nature is common with a diminished second chakra. When this chakra is overemphasized, addictions to the highs of pleasure seeking of one type or another eventually pull one down. We will first cover difficulties due to a diminished second chakra and then discuss challenges stemming from an excessive focus on this chakra.

Energy Depletion from Blocked Receptivity

Your second chakra is receptive in nature and, when blocked, leads to an energy depletion from an energetic pattern of giving more than receiving. "It is better to give than to receive" has a beautiful spiritual sound to it; however, energetically, giving more than receiving is a depletion model. If a well pumps out more water than it receives, it will run dry. The energy reservoir of your second chakra will become depleted if you always give more than you receive.

Learn to *joyfully give and joyfully receive* as a way to overcome the burnout that always comes from overgiving. There is no such thing as giving too much as long as it is matched by an equal amount of receiving.

Imagine the following scenario. A neighbor comes over to your house and asks for a minor favor, like borrowing a tool or a cooking pan. Now imagine the next day your neighbor returns the item and, carrying a bucket of soapy water, says with a big smile that he would like to wash your car. Not wanting to put him out in any way, you politely decline.

Ask yourself in this situation, while watching him walk away with his bucket, did your rejection of his offer add to the joy of the moment or diminish it? Justifications such as "he offered too much for what I did for him" support the blocking of the energy exchange, as if that were an honorable thing to do.

The teaching *pay it forward,* popularized in the 2000 movie with that title, is the antidote for keeping your energy exchanges balanced with the universe. If someone offers an act of kindness to you today, gladly accept and pay it forward by offering an act of kindness to someone else.

The act of giving often elicits joy without you needing any type of payback, like feeding birds in the winter. They will not be saying thank-you, but you can still receive great joy.

Freeing Stuck Emotional Energy

Awakening to your Higher Self doesn't free you from deep emotional patterns and wounds. A person can experience the peace of meditation and be quite awakened and aware at the spiritual level yet still be quite closed at the emotional level. Awareness helps, but awakening to the truth of your spirit still doesn't cut it when working with emotions; they don't respond to mental reasoning or a positive outlook.

Emotions are of the water element, and water needs to flow to be healthy. Emotions that are in motion are healthy. When emotions are stagnant or stuck, they are not. How do emotions become stuck? Painful memories and experiences that you have a strong resistance to will persist. That which you resist persists. In moving away from the painful memory or anything that hints of it, your aversion to it keeps it stuck.

Exercise
· ·
Liberating Blocked Emotions

It takes courage to accept certain emotions as they arise, but accepting them is what it takes to release them. The goal is not to dive back into the uncomfortable emotional state, but to stay in compassionate awareness of the uncomfortable emotion and let it wash over you and be gone, like standing in the waves of the ocean. The emotion builds, splashes over you, and is gone. *Let resisted emotions wash over you without any mental examination and without attaching to or resisting them; they come and move through you and then are gone.*

When you learn to meditate, you see this process with thoughts. Even as you vow to sit in silent awareness beyond thinking, thoughts continue to arise from the mind's effervescence. Resisting thoughts doesn't work; no matter how earnest you are in your attempts, thoughts still arise. Ultimately you learn not to resist thoughts but to simply notice them without following or analyzing them. Then they pass like a moving cloud before your inner watching.

The same practice of staying in mindful awareness of emotions as they arise without resisting, analyzing, or following them in any way allows them to move through you and subside. As you practice staying in awareness as emotions pass through you, you grow in your ability to participate in a broader range of emotional experiences with others without becoming engulfed in the emotional state.

Tenderness is required to work with emotional sensitivities—tender, compassionate awareness. Sensitivities to wounds won't come out of hiding with any "positive mental attitude" browbeating. Know that the truth of compassionate awareness will set them free, but what is required first is deep acceptance where there once was resistance. This deep acceptance liberates the emotions from their stories and allows them to flow once again.

. . . .

Emotional Responsibility and Removing Blame

Reclaiming your responsibility for your emotional well-being is of the highest priority if you are to liberate yourself from whatever is holding you back from remaining emotionally open. Although second chakra emotional issues show up early in the sequence of our exploration of the chakras from the first to the seventh, emotional freedom is often the last level most people will be able to attain. Without taking responsibility for your emotional reactions to whatever is happening to you, you stay locked in a place of no possibilities. If someone is making you feel the way you do because they did what they did, you are stuck, powerless. Knowing that no one is making you feel a particular way is the path to emotional freedom. This entails removing blame of others, or yourself, or past experiences as the cause of your current emotional state.

Envy and jealousy are annoying emotions that arise from imbalances of the second chakra. Jealousy does at least have a healthy component of protecting a relationship partner from wandering too far, but beyond that, it is toxic.

Envy has no redeeming value, and it is best to simply get over it as one of the many less-than-honorable qualities that arise from the lower chakras. When you are envious of another's possessions or position in life, you are actually sending this constricted, negative, and repelling energy toward the very thing you want. Training yourself to overcome envy by sending positive, supportive energy to those who have what you wish to have greatly enhances your magnetism and openness to attracting greater abundance into your life.

Make it a daily practice of your inner housecleaning to bless and release any feelings of envy and jealousy and rid yourself of their annoying yammering.

Excessive Second Chakra Issues

It is quite easy to get attached or addicted to the pleasures of your second chakra. Overindulgence in food, sex, alcohol, and drugs are notorious hooks that can rob a person of the simple joys of life. This quest for a constant high with no low is the basis of addiction.

With experience, you begin to realize that when you are overly attached to peak experiences, whether they be sensual or spiritual, you miss so much of the beauty of the valleys in between the peaks. Train your attention to see the beauty in the valleys and plains by looking at the minute examples of beauty right in front of you. Notice the rhythm of the grass swaying in the wind, punctuated by birds and butterflies dancing in harmonic resonance.

To return to your ability to enjoys life's simple pleasures, cultivate your interest in life's simple pleasures, like seeking out and photographing hidden treasures of beauty that you normally would not notice and would simply walk by.

Activities to Empower Your Second Chakra

Working on empowering your second chakra could hardly be called work since it is all about cultivating greater enjoyment in life—not such a bad task at all. Surrounding yourself with beauty—art, music, flowers, and whatever else might bring you joy and uplift your spirit—makes your living space itself a constant and available source for enhancing your second chakra.

Spending time near rivers, lakes, and oceans can reinvigorate your second chakra's affinity with water, as can a soothing soak in the tub or a relaxing shower. Drinking plenty of water nourishes and cleanses your second chakra, and adding orange-colored food and spices to your diet will also perk it up. Spending time under the moonlight activates the lunar nature of your second chakra, and becoming a moon watcher by tracking the phases the moon goes through each month can enhance your attunement to the cyclic nature of change.

Additional Activities
to Enhance Your Second Chakra

Yoga Postures

All hip-opener postures, such as cobbler pose and butterfly pose, are particularly effective for opening your second chakra. Cobra, forward bends, and seated pelvic circles also stimulate the flow of energy to this chakra. Breathe the color orange deep into your abdomen during your postures while picturing yourself being open to the flow of emotions moving through you.

Affirmations for Awakening Your Second Chakra

I embrace and enjoy my sensuality and sexuality.

I trust my feelings and emotions and give them room for healthy expression.

I adapt to change with ease and grace.

I have abundant opportunities for creative expression today.

Body Associations

The sexual organs, kidneys, urinary tract, spleen, bladder, gall bladder, hips, lower back, skin, and tongue are all associated with your second chakra. Difficulties in any of these areas of the body point to a need to bring this chakra into balance.

Foods for Your Second Chakra

Foods with a high water content, fruits, and all orange foods enhance your second chakra. Oranges, carrots, yams, mangoes, melons, passion fruit, juices, nuts, honey, ginger, sesame seeds, vanilla, teas, and water, water, and more water all stimulate your second chakra. Ice cream and dark chocolate are among the all-too-numerous treat foods for your pleasure chakra.

Gemstones and Crystals for the Second Chakra

Amber, orange calcite, carnelian, moonstone, citrine, and tiger's eye are beneficial for your second chakra.

Second Chakra Journaling

Before moving on to the third chakra, spend some time with your chakra journal recording your insights into how your second chakra is operating in your life and what you can do to keep it more open, balanced, and healthy. Contemplate your openness to the flow of your emotions, your adaptability to change, and your openness to your sensuality and sexuality. Record the insights you receive from your Higher Self after contemplating your experiences with your second chakra. Did you receive creative inspiration? Did you receive guidance as to how to enrich your enjoyment of life, or perhaps insights into where you need to be more disciplined with indulgences? Write these insights in your journal to greater anchor your understanding of how your second chakra is operating in your life at this time.

CHAPTER 4

Third Chakra: Manipura

Location: Solar plexus

Element: Fire

Symbol: A downward-pointing triangle within a circle with ten lotus petals

Color: Yellow

Principles: Power, transformation, metabolism

Key Benefit: A discerning use of focused willpower

Key Obstacles: A lack of drive when diminished; power conflicts when excessive

Spiritual Quality: Spiritual will aligned with the Higher Self

Type of Intelligence: Discerning intellect

Awakening to your third chakra gives you the personal power, self-esteem, and confidence to act on your choices and rise up out of complacency and make something of your life. Your third chakra is where you develop your personal power through discipline and self-control and ultimately is where you get tested with the right use of your power in the world. A balanced third chakra manifests as confidence and gives you the motivation and drive to achieve your goals.

Your third chakra activates the element of fire, energizing the transformational process of the digestive organs in their role of metabolizing food into the energy necessary to initiate action. The first arising of discernment also awakens with your third chakra, giving you the ability to make choices in your perceived best interest.

Your third chakra is your power chakra and fuels the drive to overcome insecurity, self-doubt, fear of failure, and disapproval and to rise up out of the gravitational pull of your first and second chakras. A healthy third chakra gives you motivation and the ability to be decisive and focused on your goals.

Clues that you need to activate your third chakra are feelings of being powerless, with the lack of confidence coming from a poor self-image and low self-esteem. Without the fire and will of your third chakra, the water and earth of the first two chakras become like quicksand, making it impossible to escape their grip. Lack of discernment for what is in your best interest from a weak third chakra leads to poor decision-making and difficulty concentrating, getting things done, or even taking action. A deficient solar plexus chakra also manifests as a lack of the digestive fire necessary to completely digest food, thoughts, and emotions, creating toxicity throughout the system. It takes longer to heal the wounds of life because the undigested psychological effects linger long after the wounding experience. Balancing a diminished third chakra will be discussed in the "Third Chakra Difficulties and Solutions" section later in this chapter

Self-Control and Personal Power

The ability to have self-control is an indication of the balanced alignment of your third chakra and is the source of your personal power and self-respect. When this chakra is diminished, there is a lack of self-control, and with little self-discipline, the slippery slope of immersing oneself in indulgences leads to all kinds of trouble. When the expression of your third chakra is excessive, you can be so self-controlled that it constricts the third chakra rather than opening it, leading to a lack of openness to others and essentially cutting you off from the flow of life. When excessive control issues are externalized, power is used to attempt to control and dominate others. The balanced use of this control aspect of your power chakra comes from exercising *self-control* rather than seeking to control others.

If you use this energy to whip yourself into shape, outer frustrations will dissipate. To stay sharp at whatever you are doing in life, periodic self-discipline is required to avoid losing your edge. You have to periodically discipline your desires for the sake of your health and well-being. To activate your third chakra, work proactively to achieve greater self-discipline and self-control—not just because of the warnings associated with a lack of self-control but because of how good it feels to be fit and on top of your game.

We all need some degree of unconditional self-love, but self-respect we have to earn. Where in your life could you benefit from greater self-discipline and self-control? It doesn't have to be in every area of your life, but utilize your third chakra by picking some aspect of your life that could definitely be improved with more self-imposed discipline.

A person with a balanced third chakra moves in the world with an easy confidence, and having self-respect makes it easier to respect others. When balanced in your power chakra, you can be assertive without being aggressive, not trying to prove yourself in any way.

Right Use of Power

There are two guiding principles for the right use of power. The first one, following the mandate "first, do no harm," is to *use your power in such a way that is not harmful to yourself or others.* This is the restrictive aspect of the right use of power, what not to do, and is followed by the second, proactive principle, what to do: *Use your power in such a way that is in your best interest and the best interests of others.*

Honorable Competition

With the right use of power, a person may be intensely competitive yet seek to win in an honorable way. A person with a balanced power chakra wants to win against others performing at their best. Without the mantle of honor, the competitive person takes delight when competitors make a mistake or are not able to compete at their best. With honor, this gloating over the failures of others is absent. If you are in competition with such a person, you will feel their focused intention on winning, yet at the same time you will sense that they honor your efforts.

Free Will and the Awakening of Discernment

Free will is the ability to make choices, to say yes or no, to accept a situation as is, or to make changes. Of all your personal resources, free will will have the greatest impact on your life by giving you the ability to accept the conditions you were born in or to make choices to initiate the changes necessary to transform the quality of your life. This gift of free will is always available to you in the choices you make. Even if you choose not to choose, it is your free will to do so.

Free will manifests in the choices you make throughout the day, whether they are consciously or unconsciously chosen. Unconscious choices are patterned reactions to what you say yes and no to without giving it any conscious thought. When you make a conscious choice, you use the discernment of the third chakra to assess whether a choice of action is truly in your overall best interest or not.

The mental aspect of the third chakra comes with the birth of the discerning intellect and the ability to make choices based on your own *perceived* best interest. Before awakening to the heart chakra and the awareness of your interconnectedness with others, the seat of your identity is in the lower chakras. From the lower chakras, your perceived best interest would be in making choices that support the Personal Self—period. As you awaken to a larger sense of self-identity beyond your separate Personal Self, what you perceive as your best interest expands to include the best interests of others, and your choices reflect this. But at this point on your chakra journey, it is good and appropriate to be considering only yourself.

Fire and Your Third Chakra

Fire is the element of your third chakra, and contemplating its nature adds to your understanding of your personal power. Agni is the Hindu deity associated with fire, and his attributes of energy, combustion, willpower, action, and transformation are the very nature of the third chakra.

Agni's fire transforms the gross into the subtle, as fire transforms wood into heat, smoke, and ash. As Agni is the lord of sacrificial fire, seekers would offer sacrificial offerings to him to burn in his fire, sending their requests to the deities of higher realms.

In working with your chakras, the spiritual fire at the core of your third chakra is the envoy to the higher realms of the upper chakras. When you place the offerings from your Lower Self (doubt, anger, regret, etc.) as sacrificial offerings on its flame, these are transformed from their gross vibration and purified into their higher spiritual vibrations. This is the fire of spirit that can never be extinguished, and when ignited, it purifies all that opposes clarity and is the envoy for aligning with your Higher Self.

Your third chakra is the source of your inner fire, with both its helpful and destructive potentials. When controlled, it is the fire of determination that can help you overcome bad habits and the inertia of the first two chakras. When you are wrestling with inadequacy, doubt, and other disempowering issues, work with them in your power chakra rather than your head or your heart, where they will only cause confusion.

When you are struggling with sluggish behavior, instead of trying to understand your lack of drive emotionally or mentally, take a few deep breaths into your solar plexus and picture your breath fanning its flames. Now imagine directing all of the doubt, insecurity, and lack of clarity you have been experiencing onto the flame, adding fuel to the fire. Feel the slovenly behavior being transformed in the flame into its higher energetic potential.

When fire is out of control, it can be as destructive as a forest fire, and in the personality, out-of-control fire leads to a hot, aggressive, competitive, and angry temperament. Balancing issues that arise from excessive fire will be covered in the "Third Chakra Difficulties and Solutions" section later in this chapter.

Digestive Fire and Metabolism

The fire of your third chakra is responsible for the digestion and metabolism of transforming food into energy. If the energy of your food is not fully absorbed by your solar plexus chakra, energy will not be available to distribute to the rest of the body and you will feel tired, with a lack of drive and mental clarity.

As it is in the body, so it is in the psyche. The digestive fire in the psyche transforms and metabolizes psychological and emotional experiences, removing the psychological burden of feeling guilty or shameful about past choices. As you awaken to your spiritual fire within, you can offer these unresolved wounds of the past to this inner sacrificial fire in meditation so they may be consumed in the flames and allow you to ascend to the higher realms. Just as you can offer any doubt or inadequacy issues to the transformative fire of your third chakra, you can do the same with old, haunting issues that have been lingering undigested in your psyche. Visualize directing these worthless relics that pull you out of the present to your inner fire and feel the clarity of now.

Food Choices

Digestive fire is dependent on the fuel it burns: your food. When you are unable to think clearly, it is often due to your digestive system not being able to effectively utilize the fuel it's been given.

It is not so much that "you are what you eat" as it is that you will have the amount of energy available to you based on the energy potential of the food you eat. The food you eat not only has a certain amount of physical energy available (some food has little or no vital energy or even harmful energy), but it also carries the subtle vibration of those who handled it.

Expressing thankfulness and blessing food before you eat it is always a good idea, and even more so when you eat in a public restaurant or gathering place. The energetic vibration of those who prepared and handled the food leaves a subtle imprint on the energy pattern of the food and is ingested as well. Those who grew, harvested, and shipped the food also impact the vibrational essence of the food you are about to eat. It's no wonder sensitive people often have indigestion and an unsettled stomach after dining out.

Blessing your food purifies these subtle vibrational effects, restoring its energetic essence. In a public restaurant, this can be done quite inconspicuously by cupping your hands around the side of the dish, closing your eyes for a moment, and silently expressing your gratitude for the food you are about to eat and all those who helped prepare it.

You can also support the restaurants that have arrangements with the farm-to-table movement of conscious organic farmers offering their food to local establishments. This food comes already blessed with conscious awareness.

Boundaries

All issues of boundaries arise with your solar plexus chakra. To get a sense of boundary issues, let's say you are at a gathering and are meeting someone new, and immediately the person gets too close for comfort while talking to you, triggering a gut reaction of "too close!" This is the physical sensation of your boundaries being violated. Psychologically, boundary issues show up when you are deciding how much is too much in terms of the needs, demands, and expectations of others on your energy. When are a person's needs just too much for you to deal with? This is your third chakra's boundary alarm sounding in your psyche. With no personal boundaries, one becomes adrift in life and invariably becomes a doormat for those who have a knack for seeking out boundary-less victims.

Boundary issues regularly involve saying no in one way or another, and it's best to take the high road and do this in a way that honors your energy field and doesn't wound others. Life is filled with situations where others make demands of you or express needs that require your attention. There are some situations where the needs of others require you to do something that you might not ordinarily choose to do. Let's say an elderly parent needs to move and no one else is available to help. You might choose to sacrifice your personal desires for the weekend to offer your services, and after making the sacrifice, you feel good about your choice. There was something honorable about the sacrifice.

However, there are many requests made of you where, even after making the personal sacrifice to fulfill the request, you don't feel that you did something honorable—quite the contrary. Instead, you feel taken advantage of and dishonored, disrespected. These are the requests that you want to weed out, and only your saying no will end these less-than-honorable energy drains. Plus, it feels great to say yes to honoring your boundaries by saying no to that which dishonors you. "That is not going to work for me. I have other issues that require my attention that I need to tend to." This simple statement is truthful and honors your energy field, and is all that is required.

Service/Servant

The service/servant phenomenon is a boundary issue. When you are being of service, you are gladly offering your energy to the task at hand. Being a servant is when your service is expected, but it doesn't feel like a glad offering at all! Let's say you're volunteering with a particular group you choose to support with your efforts. Being of service feels good, but what happens when you have reached the limit of what you can joyfully give and you now have other things to attend to in your life? To keep going past the point of giving joyfully is draining. You start feeling like a servant, asking yourself questions such as, "How much do they expect of me? How much do they think I can do? When will they tell me I've done enough?"

Wrong questions. This is the question that needs to be asked to clearly define the boundary between being of service and being a servant: "When will I set my boundary of how much I can give and when enough is enough?" Only you can define the boundaries of what you need to maintain a healthy life.

If a person has not yet integrated their third chakra and is nevertheless trying to surrender to a greater power than the personal will, their personal life will be problematic. If "not by my will, but by thy will" means totally abdicating personal responsibility for making discerning choices, you haven't shown up for the tests upon your personal power chakra and your personal life will suffer the consequences.

Third Chakra
for the Spiritually Inclined

Before awakening to your spiritual will, an effective third chakra is the fire in the belly of your personal will and expresses outward into worldly activity. Picture your spiritual will as the core of the fire of your personal will, an intense flame that is directed upward, not outward. Your spiritual will seeks to align with the higher spiritual realms, and this takes effort of a different sort—the effort to rise above the petty, the dross, and the denser aspects of your life. Present the less-than-honorable lower aspects of yourself as offerings on the sacrificial fire of your spiritual will to be transformed into their higher energetic potential.

Let's say you have been seeking to be aligned with your soul's purpose, and in meditation you have been asking your Higher Self for guidance. Imagine that your Higher Self responds to your prayers, giving you an inspired project to take on that your Lower Self has doubts about your ability to achieve. This is when you want to call on your spiritual will to assist you in rising up out of your doubts and feelings of inadequacy to answer the call of your soul's purpose.

A quote about humility from Rick Warren's book *The Purpose-Driven Life* is helpful to consider when the question arises of "who am I to pursue such a lofty goal?"

Humility isn't thinking less of yourself;
it's thinking of yourself less. [2]

Thinking about yourself less is the way. When you are confronted with the question of "who do I think I am to pursue this direction?" a response from your spiritual will would be, "Who are you not to follow your soul's promptings?" Get your concerns and questions about inadequacy out of the way to follow your soul's calling.

In meditation, take all the doubts and feelings of inadequacy that arise from the ego, place them on the fire of your spiritual will, and picture yourself taking the steps toward your soul's calling.

Spiritual Warrior

A spiritual warrior is not fighting outer battles nor sounding the trumpet for spiritual causes in the world. A spiritual warrior is fighting the battle within that must be won every day to rise up out of the pull of the lower chakras and their all-too-human hungers, needs, and desires. Spiritual will is necessary to maintain the steadfast dedication it takes to make progress in rising above the less-than-honorable aspects of being in a human body.

Third Chakra
Difficulties and Solutions

Difficulties with the third chakra come from either its excessive or its diminished expression. First we'll cover the excessive, too-much-fire-in-the-belly issues, and then the difficulties from having a diminished third chakra.

---

2. Rick Warren, *The Purpose-Driven Life* (Grand Rapids, MI: Zondervan, 2002).

Excessive Power Chakra Issues

An excessive emphasis on one's third chakra is just as common as an underdeveloped one and can manifest as power conflicts, having hot-tempered anger outbursts, being competitive in inappropriate situations, and acting defensively, with excessive sensitivity to any criticism. Too much fire comes across as willful, even intimidating at times—whatever it takes to get one's way and stay in control.

If you are working on taming the overly self-protective nature of your third chakra, the residual behavior patterns of being overly defensive may still show up, interfering with interactions with others. If you are conscious of this defensiveness and are working at removing it from your character and yet you find yourself reacting in an overly defensive way, try acknowledging it to the other person. "I know I appear defensive, and I'm working on this, but I really want to hear what you have to say, so please continue." By acknowledging your conscious awareness of your behavior, the other person will no longer be as put off by your reaction, and the constricted energy will dissolve.

Excessive focus on one's power chakra most often comes from validating one's self-worth exclusively through external achievements. This is quite common in a culture such as ours that places such high value on success and status. At the extreme are the manipulative power trippers who use intimidation and explosive anger to get their way. More commonly, excessive power is seen in those who tend to be overly competitive with inappropriate people in inappropriate situations, hypercritical of others, or in a constant rant of their disapproval of one thing or another.

Those who are locked in the grip of winning at all costs rarely see this as a problem; they are the ones who are winning, after all, at least in their minds! It is not until a person experiences that all this winning has led to losing in so many other areas of life—such as health, relationships, and well-being—that they realize how much has been sacrificed upon the altar of success. It is not until a person essentially crashes and burns from too much effort that the need becomes apparent to cultivate other aspects of life outside of success in the quest to have a meaningful life.

Practice
. . . .
Gaining Control of Excessive Power

If you are coming into the awareness that you want to gain more control of your power chakra, by noticing that you are too hot-headed and prone to argument more than you wish, it is your awareness of this that is your greatest resource. If you can stay in your awareness even as a power conflict or argument arises, that gap between your awareness and the heat arising in your solar plexus is all you need. That little gap of awareness allows free will, choice. When you are locked into the reaction with no awareness, your free will is gone and there is no ability to make choices.

Staying in mindful awareness allows you to notice the tightness in your solar plexus that attends an upcoming power conflict such as an argument. Whatever you say when your solar plexus is hot and tight will be heard as hot and tight and will trigger a defensive reaction due to the perceived hostile energy. Speech begins in your solar plexus, and words born of a hot, tight solar plexus will carry this vibration.

To affirm that speech begins in your solar plexus, place your hand lightly on your solar plexus and say a word. Notice how your third chakra pulsates with the sound of the word like a piano string stretched between your solar plexus and your mouth forming the words. Notice that the vibration is initiated with your solar plexus. The vibration of words, the "vibes" of what you are saying, is initiated in your third chakra.

Staying in mindful awareness of this, first breathe deep into your belly with the intention of cooling and softening the hot, tight ball of energy you feel when angry. This is particularly important when you have a valid issue that needs to be confronted and yet you don't want to sabotage the discussion by appearing hot and tight. This essentially calms your energy, at least somewhat, before an important discussion.

Angry, hot, volatile energy can also be transformed into its positive polarity with the following exercise.

Exercise
. . . .
Transmutation of Negative Energy

Whenever you are mad, angry, irritated, or frustrated, there is a surge of the fiery energy of your third chakra. It is energy for sure, but it is negative, destructive fire. We like energy, but we don't like all of its negative manifestations. This energy can be transmuted into its positive polarity using the sacrificial fire of your spiritual will.

The first step in the transmutation of negative energy is to reclaim your direct experience of the energy by removing all blame. Where is the source of the power in the statement "I am mad because of what he or she did or didn't do"? In this statement, the source of your experience of being mad is the other person; thus, that person holds all of the power to cause you to feel this way. You have given away your power, and the first step is to reclaim your direct experience of being mad by removing whatever label you have for its cause.

Remove the label by stopping the statement at "I am mad." Period. Not because of anything. You are simply mad. Now you have claimed responsibility for the experience of the energy. Now it is yours and you can work with it. When the source of your experience is labeled as outside of you, you have no power to work with it. You've given it away to what happened and that is that. But if you reclaim your power by owning the direct experience of being angry, then it is yours to work with—the first step in reclaiming your power.

After reclaiming your power by removing the labels, picture yourself gathering all of this hot, negative energy into a seething, molten ball of dark energy in your gut, where you feel this energy. Breathe deep into the image of this molten mass of dark energy and pull it deeper into the core of your solar plexus chakra and the radiant fire of your spiritual will. Picture all of the darkness and negative energy being burned away, leaving clear, radiant, unattached energy.

Now you can do anything you want with the energy, such as work out, play, or engage in a creative project. It is your energy now. It is the same powerful energy, but with all the negative energy transformed into its positive potential. It is still energy, so you must direct it into self-directed activity or it will likely seek another negative outlet. If the energy is not consciously directed, you may find that you are no longer mad at what he did, but now you are mad at what the neighbors did! No gain. That is why it is important to direct the energy into some positive activity once it has been transmuted.

. . . .

Mentor or Critic?

When you really do see a better way for someone to handle a particular task and you have the authority of experience to warrant your perspective, how do you relay the information to the other person? Are you a mentor or a critic? When you think back to high school or college and remember who your favorite teachers were, ask yourself, were they mentors or critics in the way they handled their authority with you? Likely, they were mentors, those who saw how you could improve your skills and yet made you feel confident that you could do so. They empowered you with their guidance.

The critics, on the other hand, disempowered you with their hypercritical disapproval of your performance. If you sincerely want to be helpful for another person, be mindful of whether you are being a mentor or a critic in your delivery, and your effectiveness will improve dramatically.

Resistance Fuels Separateness, Acceptance Fuels Unity

Being overly controlled leads to resistance in the personality. Resistance can always be felt as a tightness and a constriction in your solar plexus. Resistance shows up when you are projecting your mental image of how you think the world ought to be and it simply isn't like that! Life, in one way or another, is not unfolding the way you think it should.

Applying the principle of "that which you pay attention to grows," you realize that to be against something adds fuel to its existence. Awakening liberates your life force energy from being expended in needless resistance. You start becoming aware of the expense of resistance on your energy field and start preferring not to invest your energy in these reactionary energy drains. Awakening creates a little space between stimulus and reaction, and you have greater freedom in choosing what to invest your life force in.

Practice
. . . .
If You Are Going to Do It, Choose to Do It!

Resisting that which you have no control over is an argument with life itself, and it is best just to let go of this type of resistance. Being in resistance to activities you are engaged in is exhausting rather than engaging and can be turned around.

When you are engaged in an activity to which you have resistance, your will and energy become fragmented and the task feels burdensome. If you are going to do a task anyway and it needs to get done whether you like it or not, choose to like it, or at least choose to do it, and you will not be divided within yourself.

. . . .

Entering into Activity Rather Than Doing It

It can be exhausting when your entire life seems to depend on the strength of your will, and even if you are successful, it can feel like you are pushing your life up a hill. Exhaustion from your third chakra comes from expending too much effort even though that is what it seems to require to be successful.

As you awaken to the right use of will and there are genuine needs to be met and tasks to be done calling for your action, choosing to enter into the activity rather than *doing* it removes self-imposed resistances. If the needs are authentic and you've chosen right activity, there is a subtle vortex of energy within the need itself that you can draw on by interacting with the need to bring it to completion. In interacting with the activity rather than just imposing your will on it, you draw on the energy of interaction with the activity. Lao-Tzu's teachings on *wu wei*, the path of effortless action, supports this and is expressed poetically in verse 37 of the *Tao Te Ching*: "The Tao does nothing, yet leaves nothing undone."

Diminished Third Chakra Difficulties

A diminished third chakra leads to feelings of being powerless, a lack of confidence coming from a poor self-image and low self-esteem. Lack of discernment for what is in your best interest from a weak third chakra leads to poor decision-making and difficulty concentrating, getting things done, or even taking action.

How to activate

Feeling worthless, unsure, and hesitant are also signs of a weak power chakra. Any challenge can seem intimidating, and your outlook on life becomes dim and grim without the brightness of internal fire.

The paradox of having a weak third chakra is that what is needed to increase the fire in your belly is willpower, the very thing that is missing in a diminished power chakra. Compassion for the dilemma aside, what is needed to get moving is physical exercise. Begin with a walk and work toward fitness, along with maintaining a disciplined diet that stokes your fire and eliminates that which sedates it. You can't wait for the energy to build to take action; you must will yourself into action, exercising self-control, the source of the power of your third chakra.

Victim Consciousness

Victim consciousness is any type of belief that other people are to blame for your situation in life. There are true victims in life who have experienced violent abuse from others, and our hearts reach out to them for the strength and love they will need to get over the shock trauma from these experiences. Those who go on to heal themselves from the wounds of abuse and lead healthy, successful lives do so by finding the source of strength within themselves that is stronger than the wounds inflicted on them.

Your spiritual will is stronger than any wrongs that have been done to you. As you regain your connection to this source of power and light at the center of your solar plexus, it purifies past karma and you begin to be more informed by the light, strength, and clarity that arises with the use of your spiritual will. Past wounding experiences no longer define you in any way and become experiences you have gone through but are not you.

Fear of Failure

Fear of failure is a manifestation of a weak third chakra. Inability to follow through and complete goals and projects is often caused by an underlying avoidance of possible failure. As you strengthen your power chakra, fear of failure abates, to be replaced by the fear of not living up to the fullest of your potential. A fear of missing out on life fuels the courage to try things you were once too timid to consider.

When you are first overcoming a fear of failure and are considering backing down on some opportunity, instead of making your choice based on fear, ask yourself, "Which option will empower me and which one will not?" Choose the path that will empower you and then use your willpower to follow through. Even if you are not successful at achieving your goal, you will still feel the honor that comes from trying.

Inability to Express Anger

Many people have difficulty expressing the honest anger they do feel. Obviously, it is better not to be carrying anger at all, but there are times when its expression brings needed clarity to a relationship, while the inability to express this honest anger leads to a lack of clarity. Whether the reason for your excessive aversion to anger stems from early childhood experiences or from a moral commitment to renounce anger, the inability to express the honest anger that arises in life will manifest in unconscious and unhealthy ways. Passive-aggressive behavior, lacing your conversation with barbs rather than giving voice to the actual issue, or expressing your anger at the wrong person are examples of unconscious expression of anger.

If you have difficulty expressing the genuine anger that does arise in the course of living with others, although the anger is unexpressed, it is still in your energy field and is very evident to others. When others ask if something is bothering you, they are responding to your energy field, not to what is being said or not said. With blocked anger, you are not being honest about the true condition of your energy field, and it confuses others. They can feel that you are upset or angry, yet you are claiming that everything is fine.

Of course it is not advisable to give voice to every little thing that bothers you, but if the inability to express anger is a pattern in your life, it can lead to a lack of clarity. It takes courage to speak your truth, and this can feel risky, like you might be initiating hostilities. The benefit of expressing honest anger is that it brings clarity. Maybe your issue is warranted, and by bringing it out in the open, you might educate others as to something they might not have been aware of and clarity can be restored. Or perhaps when your anger is brought to light, you might discover that your issue really doesn't have merit and recognize that the lack of clarity was on your part, which again brings clarity.

Activities to Empower Your Third Chakra

Setting goals to achieve something is a sure method of focusing your will. Your goals can be personal, such as improved fitness or financial, professional, recreational, or creative projects, but having a goal of one type or another to aspire to strengthens your power chakra. Nothing builds confidence and self-esteem faster than success, so build in realistic benchmarks that you can be successful at on the way to your ultimate goal.

Getting direct sunlight during outdoor activities empowers your fire chakra, as does sitting around a campfire or fireplace. Meditating on the flame of a candle while contemplating your inner fire is another technique for activating your third chakra.

Physical exercise that focuses on core strength building, such as sit-ups, stomach crunches, and kettle bell swinging from the abdomen, directly benefits your solar plexus chakra. For those who practice yoga, postures that strengthen the core—such as boat pose, forward lunges, salute to the sun, and warrior pose—empower your third chakra, as does aerobically vigorous yoga such as Ashtanga.

Additional Activities to Enhance Your Third Chakra

Third Chakra Breathing: Breath of Fire

On the inbreath, pull the air deep into your abdomen and let your belly swell with the expanded air. On the outbreath, forcibly expel the air from your belly by tightening your diaphragm and pulling your stomach in, hollowing it toward your spine. Do this bellows breathing rapidly, picturing your breath fanning the flame of your third chakra and igniting your will.

Affirmations for Empowering Your Third Chakra

I will do my best today. I will rise above that which would hold me back, internally and externally, and put forth my best effort.

I ignite the fire of my spiritual will and throw all my doubts, fears, and insecurities into this fire, transforming them into pure energy.

If I learn as much from every mistake as I do from every success, there will never be failure.

I choose to align my will with the callings of my Higher Self.

Body Associations

The digestive system (including the large intestine, stomach, and diaphragm), the process of metabolism, and the liver, pancreas, muscular system, adrenal cortex, and eyes are all associated with your third chakra. Difficulties with any of these areas of the body indicate an imbalance in your third chakra.

Third Chakra Foods

Foods that sustain digestive fire and are processed slowly, such as complex carbohydrates and whole grains, as well as all yellow foods stimulate the digestive fire of your third chakra. Granola, rice, quinoa, buckwheat, flax, yellow squash, yellow lentils, corn, yellow peppers, sweet bananas, pineapple, cheeses, yogurt, sunflower seeds, curry, turmeric, cumin, and fennel all enhance your third chakra. Popcorn and nachos with peppers are recreational food options for activating the fire of your third chakra.

Third Chakra Journaling

This would be a good time to reflect on your third chakra insights, before proceeding to the fourth chakra and getting introduced to a new range of material. Record your insights into how you can enhance your personal power chakra in your chakra journal. Note your strengths and the ways in which you would like to improve your use of your power.

CHAPTER 5

Fourth Chakra: Anahata

Location: Upper chest behind the heart

Element: Air

Symbol: Two interlacing upward and downward triangles within a circle with twelve lotus petals

Colors: Green and pink

Principle: Love at the personal, compassionate, and universal levels

Key Benefits: Acceptance of others and openness to life

Key Obstacles: Attachment and grief

Spiritual Quality: Loving-kindness toward others born of compassionate acceptance of the spiritual essence at the core of all beings

Type of Intelligence: Compassionate

Your fourth chakra, *anahata* in Sanskrit, is located in your upper chest behind your heart and is most often referred to as your heart chakra. Love at the personal, compassionate, and spiritual levels is experienced with the awakening of your heart chakra. You shift from reaching for love from the lower chakras to giving from love at your awakened fourth chakra. Love as something to acquire, as if it were a noun, changes to love as a verb, something to do.

Anahata awakens the qualities of selfless love, empathy, compassion, altruism, and, at the spiritual level, devotion, while also awakening your capacity to experience grief and sorrow over losses. The *love of power* from the third chakra transforms to the *power of love* at the fourth chakra.

With the awakening of your heart chakra, you rise up out of your identity with your Personal Self and the sense of being separate from all others to realize that you are part of a larger reality, woven together through a vast web of relationships extending from you into all of creation. From the first stirrings of the "I" becoming part of a "we" that awaken with personal love, to the stirrings of compassionate concern for others, to the love of the spiritual essence behind all of creation, your heart chakra connects you to a larger reality.

When you experience life with an open heart chakra, you feel an abundance of love, peace, and meaningful connections with others and the world around you. Life seems to flow through you as you awaken to your heart chakra's orientation of acceptance, shedding the personal judgments and resistances of your lower chakras. You experience an essential paradigm shift as you awaken to a world beyond the limited perspective of your lower chakras, with greater acceptance of the world and others being the key that dramatically changes the quality of your engagement with life.

Anahata in Sanskrit translates as unstruck, unheard, or unhurt, as a bell remaining unrung. It is the place deep within your heart beneath the personal wounds that has never been hurt by life. This may seem counterintuitive, because people who come from their hearts often get their hearts broken. Your fourth chakra is the bridge between your lower and upper chakras, allegiant to both. It goes through the pain of losses in your personal life but is also where you have access to your spiritual heart. Your spiritual heart is transcendent and detached from the personal and is the source of causeless love, joy, and *agape* (giving from the inexhaustible divine source of love). Causeless love flows from the inexhaustible source within and is not based on any conditions whatsoever. When you are the source of love, there is no need to gather love—it comes from an inexhaustible source and is always available.

Awakening to your heart chakra gives you the ability to make decisions outside the tugs and pulls of the ego's wants and desires. The voices from the lower chakras are "unheard," and thus selfless love is born, free of the needs, desires, and attachments of the lower chakras.

The symbol for the heart chakra of two interlacing triangles, one pointing up and the other down, is the symbol of the marriage of heaven and earth within the center of your being. The integration of all polarities occurs in your heart: the union of your Higher Self and your Personal Self, male/female, yin/yang, physical/spiritual, and the pure animating spirit of the divine entwined with the fertile womb of nature.

The interlacing triangles reveal your heart chakra's allegiance to both your upper and your lower chakras. This chakra expresses itself in personal love and can also rise above personal feelings to experience the detached love of spirit, honoring the divine in all beings. The heart chakra drawing from above sees and honors the eternal, unwounded spirit behind the rising and falling of personal joys and sorrows. Even in the mourning of the death of a loved one, the personal sorrow of the loss is felt, as well as lightness for the spirit of the loved one set free from human limitations.

There is the possibility in your heart chakra to rise up to the higher vibration of selfless love and the liberated consciousness that comes from deep acceptance, but the inverted triangle reveals how vulnerable you are to slipping back down into the lower chakras and their fearful perspective. Which will you choose? This is the battle that must be won every day to stay anchored in the heart. Will you make your choices from the fear born of your lower chakras or from the faith in the power of love from your heart chakra? Will you choose the constricted energy of fear or the expansive energy of love? Choose love to stay in your heart chakra.

A simple test to use to see if you are coming from your heart or not is to ask yourself, "Am I making my choices from fear or love?" Even when considering something you do that is good for you, such as eating a healthy diet, ask yourself, "Am I doing this out of a fear of illness or a love of feeling healthy?" It is the same activity, yet your approach to it has a very different impact on your health and well-being. Doing things out of fear weakens rather than strengthens your energy field, while acting from your heart empowers your vitality in all ways.

It takes courage to live from one's heart when fears are so dominant in the world. The word *courage* comes from the Latin *cor*, meaning "heart." We often think of courage as performing heroic acts of bravery from one's power chakra; however, it is the power of one's heart that drives courageous action. Everyday heroic acts of courage that might be less newsworthy but are just as dramatic in their impact are evidenced in the addict who overcomes the destructive habit to live a healthy life and in the person who grew up in a violent household yet overcomes the impulse to strike his own children.

When you are coming from your heart, your kindness and compassion allow others to feel safe to be themselves in your presence. Others sense your accepting nature and feel at ease to drop their defenses, knowing they won't be judged. Your loving, caring nature warms the souls of those you touch, and you inspire a higher level of discourse in your interactions with others.

Your heart chakra awakens your ability to express your thoughts and feelings in a way that touches the hearts of others. Speech is initiated in your third chakra, passing through your fourth chakra before being expressed at your fifth chakra. With an open heart chakra, your speech takes on a lyrical quality, drawing others away from their concerns. Poetry, music, writing, and painting are potential outlets for the refined energy of the fourth chakra, as is connecting deeply with others.

Everyone has access to their heart. If a healthy life and loving relationships were to be found only in the mind, then only really smart people could find their way to love. Fortunately, the heart doesn't require a degree, special skills, physical prowess, or any other special qualification. The heart doesn't even need to fully understand others to love them.

We will explore the three levels of personal, compassionate, and spiritual love, but first we will explore the nature of your heart chakra and the paradigm shift that comes from its awakening.

The *fear, scarcity, and lack* mentality of the lower chakras shifts to a *faith, acceptance, and abundance* orientation with the awakening of your heart chakra. This shift radically transforms your experience of life. While others may experience the day with concerns for their safety, security, and unmet desires, you experience the same day as abundantly fulfilling.

When your heart chakra opens, you shift from wanting life to be a certain way to accepting others as they are and life as it is. While your lower chakras look at life with a fear of there not being enough of what you want and an equal fear of losing what you are attached to, your heart chakra looks at life as a field of abundant opportunities to experience the bounty of life with others.

The Power of the Heart

The power of love is the ability to win the hearts and minds of others. You can gain the obedience of others and control them with the power of intimidation and fear, but you won't earn their allegiance that way. If you win people's hearts, you gain their loyalty.

As the center of your chakra system, your heart chakra receives, integrates, and synthesizes all the information from all the other chakras; thus, it determines the dominant energetic tone of your being. The heart is also by far the strongest generator of electromagnetic energy in the body.

We are learning from quantum physics that the physical world, including our bodies, is made up more of packets of energy than of bits of matter. Since your heart is your largest generator of electromagnetic energy, the energy field of your heart chakra is going to have the greatest impact on the health of your body and mind and your relationships with the world around you.

A Heart Story
That Which Is Born of Love Will Be Lovely

There was a time when I was first getting to know my wife Laurie, over forty years ago now, when I was at a major crossroads in my life. We were both in Teacher Corps, in training to become elementary school teachers. When I first met Laurie at our orientation meeting, something fired off in me.

It's not that I heard bells—it was deeper than that. I couldn't call it a deep knowing, because it was quite unfamiliar. It was more like a deep wanting to know this energy that was awakening. We were both in committed, long-term relationships, and along with being schoolteachers in a small town, there was plenty of expected protocol as to what was proper as we got to know each other. Yet our magnetism knew no protocol, and even the schoolchildren could feel it and would spontaneously sing songs on the playground about us "kissing in the trees."

I had been wrestling with these two voices of protocol and my heart's desire for nearly the two years of our training when I came to the tipping point. I remember specifically the moment I was about to plunge into all-in, and I was all too aware of the protocol that was about to be violated and the myriad changes that would come from jumping into an uncertain future. I remember the moment of that awareness, and I heard my Higher Self's guidance: "Trust your heart and know that which is born of love will be lovely." And we took the step together.

We have been blessed with an abundant life, decidedly not in accordance with accepted protocol, and I have no doubt it has been from following the voice of love. We feel lucky in the rather magical life that has unfolded for us, and I have no doubt we most definitely are, and have been, most fortunate. I have grown to realize that luck and love are intimately connected. Love manifests as good fortune in life.

. . . .

Heartmind

The heart and the mind are in a constant dialogue, with much more information being sent from the heart to the mind than is popularly believed. Experientially, the following examples reveal just how often your heart sends the message of what your brain will look for: An angry heart leads to an angry mind. A suspicious heart leads to a suspicious mind. A peaceful heart leads to a peaceful mind. A loving heart leads to a loving mind. A closed heart leads to closed mind. A wounded heart leads to a wounded mind.

That the mind also drives the heart is easy to demonstrate by intentionally directing the mind to a painful memory and observing how the emotions associated with the previous experience can arise as if the experience were current. There is a two-way, symbiotic flow of information between the head and the heart. Thought and emotion combined manifest as the feelings we hold in our heart. Together, they create a blended energetic vibration that emanates from our heart and that life coalesces around.

We think of the heart and the head as separate: "My head thinks this way, but my heart feels another way." As the two become unified, coherence develops and they function as heartmind, functioning not just simultaneously but also synergistically, with greater capacity in their unified state than when they are together side by side.

Coherence and the Attitude of Gratitude

Coherence is the energy you feel when your mind and heart are aligned. The surest way to experience coherence directly is by contemplating the people you are most thankful for in your life or situations in your life of which you are deeply appreciative. This always works to bring the heart and mind into energetic harmony.

It doesn't take but a few minutes of practicing the attitude of gratitude to shift your energy into a heart-based focus. This centers the mind and creates coherence in your energy field, integrating the heart-mind system so that they work together. When you are in personal coherence, even your silent presence creates energetic resonance within others. You become like a tuning fork that raises the vibration of those in your presence.

Your Heart's Role in Exhaustion

When you are experiencing exhaustion and depleted energy, you might first rightly consider your third chakra and your adrenals. However, along with your solar plexus chakra, you should also consider your heart chakra's role in your experience of energy.

The poet David Whyte tells a story in his book *Crossing the Unknown Sea* about asking a religious scholar friend his thoughts on exhaustion. They were getting together for an evening of translating poetry while enjoying a glass of wine. Whyte was exhausted by the time his friend arrived, and as they settled in, he asked his question concerning exhaustion. The monk's response was illuminating: "The antidote to exhaustion is not necessarily rest. The antidote for exhaustion is wholeheartedness."

You know this experientially in the difference you feel when you are trying to get through an activity that your heart is just not engaged in compared to the energy you feel when your heart is involved. When your heart is not involved, there is no energetic exchange between you and whatever you are doing. It's all output, and exhaustion is inevitable.

When contemplating this teaching of why you might be experiencing exhaustion in some area of your life, the question becomes, why is your heart not engaged in the activity that is depleting your energy field? Is it that the resistance is within you and you have to get your head out of the way to put your heart into the activity? Or is it that the container you are trying to pour your heart into isn't large enough to accommodate all you have to give? Of course we are not just talking about projects but also relationships. It's a tough question, but the right one.

Personal Love and Intimacy

As the first chakra above your lower chakras, your heart chakra is where you first expand your sense of self to include those you love, where the "I" first becomes part of a "we." This is where you are first awakened to *caring* for another—not just desiring but caring for another's well-being.

Beyond romance, your heart chakra seeks intimacy in close relationships. Intimacy comes from being with others in such a way that it is safe to drop all armor and knowing that they have dropped their armor as well; you merge together to discover the moment. This is the nectar of intimacy, and it requires deep trust to feel safe enough to drop all defenses to get to this deepest level of connecting with another.

Hungry Heart

There are times when you might experience a hungry heart due to a lack of intimacy in even your closest relationships. There are many potential reasons for experiencing this lack, most dealing with feeling a lack of safety in dropping all armor, the prerequisite for intimacy. Keeping an open heart in ongoing relationships also requires the ability to forgive.

"Forgive everybody for everything" would be the heart chakra's motto for living life, and it would be wonderful if just having this attitude worked. However, forgiveness requires more than an attitude adjustment and most often requires self-inquiry as to your role in what you are forgiving.

I have been married for over forty years and have had many opportunities to learn about forgiveness. When my wife and I have gone through a difficulty that requires forgiveness, I have learned that simply forgiving her is not enough. It is a change of heart that sets the stage for healing; but until I've done my inner work, the armor prevails.

My armor persists until I've examined my role in the issue at hand and ask the tough questions of my Higher Self: What was my role in the difficulty? How can I be a better person by working on some part of my character to handle this situation more skillfully? Where can I learn to be a more caring, compassionate, and wise partner for my wife? When I see my role and what I can work on within myself, I feel the armor come down and I can have an open heart again.

Another reason that couples fall out of intimacy in long-term relationships is because they know each other too well. When we know a person so well that we get lulled into believing there is nothing new to discover, intimacy disappears. Intimacy can only be discovered fresh in the moment, and when you know a person too well, you begin to relate to what you already know about your partner and opportunities for discovery vanish.

J. Krishnamurti said something to the effect that "the day you teach the child the name of the bird, the child will never see that bird again." This teaching implies that when you label something, discovery ends. Before the child knows the name for "bird," seeing one in flight thrills the child with wonder and discovery. With the naming of the bird, the teaching is that from now on the child will see it and name it, and now "knowing" the bird, will have no need for fresh discovery.

This teaching reveals why believing that we already know someone prevents us from discovering the evolving, changing, growing, alive presence of the close people in our lives in this moment.

Regaining Intimacy with Life

When your heart is open in a relationship, there is a quality of aliveness to the relationship that comes from interacting with the living presence of your partner in the here and now. An open heart doesn't need to understand another person to love them. It does so on a level beyond the rational, self-serving mind and loves without understanding, enjoying discovering the mystery of the other. You start listening to others from a state of being lovingly present and not just waiting to say your piece. You choose to love and understand more than focusing on your need to be loved and understood.

When this intimate connection with your partner is missing, the love becomes stagnant. The danger in a long-term relationship is in drifting into the illusion that you already know your partner. When we know someone only with the mind, information from the emotional and intuitive faculties is cut off, and most importantly, the keen edge of discovery is missing, and exchanges become patterned and lacking the possibility of intimacy.

The danger of believing you know someone too well is that you then are essentially in a relationship with your idea of them, a mental image of the other person. This works in much the same way as naming the bird for the child; you can fall into the trap of believing that you already "know" the people in your life and then your idea of who they are becomes what you are in a relationship with, missing the aliveness of the moment and the possibility for discovery.

Practice

. . . .

Approach Your Partner as a Mystery
to Regain Intimacy

Approach your partner as a mystery to discover to keep the aliveness in your relationship. The lower chakras approach others in terms of your needs, wants, and desires. We want others to be as we think they should be, imposing our lower chakra perspective and judgments onto them. As you awaken to heart chakra love, you no longer need to understand another person to love them. With the heart, separateness melts with the flow of shared interconnected love.

When faced with the quandary of not understanding your partner in some way, ask yourself what it is that you really value. Is it experiencing the flow of love or fully understanding your partner? Notice the moment when you have a judgment or strong opinion about how you want your partner to change. When you engage those thoughts in your mind, ask yourself, what is the energetic feeling connected to these thoughts? You will notice that it is not the feeling of love at all—these thoughts take you out of your heart. Make the choice in that moment to choose love, if that is what you value the most. This will open your heart and you will be back in the flow, and judgments will fall away on their own.

. . . .

Self-Love and Acceptance

It is commonly understood how important self-love is in allowing the love of another in your life. "You can only love another to the degree that you love yourself" is often heard in this regard, but what does it mean to love one's self? It certainly goes beyond looking in a mirror and cultivating feelings of love and admiration for the person you see looking back at you. It is not your ego loving its own reflection that awakens at the heart chakra; it is your Higher Self's love, acceptance, and gratitude for this human life you have been blessed with. The deep acceptance of your humanness and your frailties comes from the heart chakra being aligned with your spiritual self, your Higher Self.

Practicing self-love is particularly important if you have feelings of self-hatred or self-loathing. This leads to feelings of disgust with yourself and feeling unworthy of being loved and accepted, particularly if someone were to discover how terrible you are beneath the surface and all the bad things you have done in the past.

The proverb "To err is human, to forgive divine"[3] needs to be employed to open a heart filled with self-loathing from past misdeeds. If not self-love, then at least self-acceptance is a necessary first step in healing your heart chakra. Tune in to your Higher Self, and from there, radiate compassion, acceptance, and love to your Lower Self as you would to a long-time friend or child, despite the mistakes they have made.

Exercise
. . . .
Having Council with Your Higher Self

You could develop a practice of having council with your Higher Self at the end of each day. Council is safe territory to speak and hear truth. Sit with your Higher Self and review

___

3. Alexander Pope, *An Essay on Criticism* (1711; reprint, Leicester, UK: Scolar Press, 1970).

your day with an open heart and an eye for where you can improve in all of your involvements with others. Ask your Higher Self, "What are today's lessons on how I can still improve in living from my heart?" Your Higher Self is a mentor, not a critic, and accepts your Lower Self unconditionally, not holding you in judgment even when you blow it. Being willing to learn from your Higher Self each and every day will help you avoid making today's mistakes into tomorrow's problems. Clear your conscience each night to start each day with an open heart. This is an excellent time for journaling the insights you have gained from having council with your Higher Self.

. . . .

Compassionate Love

On the spiritual path, we learn to detach into the refuge of the Observer within, where we are untouched by the joys and sorrows of the world and are simply aware. There is great peace in this. Resting in the conscious awareness that we are the awareness, and are not what we are currently aware of, is the surest way to pull out of the agonies that our ego puts us through. There is peace in this detachment, but it can become a little dry, even lonely. Constantly detaching from life feels a bit like the Hermit card in the tarot, holding the light of truth but being alone on the mountaintop.

Why not just stay in this peaceful, detached place once you've found your piece of heaven? It is often compassion that pulls us back into the world. It is the compassionate heart chakra that compels us to do what we can to help alleviate the needless suffering in the world. There are many hardships and difficulties in the natural flow of life, with challenges such as aging, illness, and death that can't be avoided. The awakened heart has compassion for this but also sees the needless suffering that exists and wants to do something about it.

As your heart continues to open, your kindhearted nature naturally reaches out to help ease the suffering of others during trying or difficult times. Although a person with an open heart cannot necessarily shield themselves from their awareness of the pain and suffering of others, they can learn how to become skillfully compassionate. Carrying the burdens of others as if they were your own is unskillful because it essentially is adding to the suffering in the world rather than diminishing it. Skillful compassion is touching the pain of others with genuine care, feeling it within yourself, and then releasing it with a prayer of healing.

Practice
. . . .
Releasing Others from
Your Energy Field

When you feel emotionally drained from carrying other people's burdens and worrying about their difficulties, try the practice of "feel it, bless it, release it" (from chapter 3) even for a few minutes and you will find how often this helps you pull up out of the emotional burden you've been carrying and gives you the feeling you've done something helpful. You might still be aware of the pain and suffering of others, but you will no longer be carrying the heavy load as if it were your own.

Another method for breaking the connection in a healthy way after interacting with someone who is drawing too much energy from you is a technique healers learn to close their sessions. Healers, energy workers, and those who give readings for others learn the importance of intentionally closing the connection after a deep session with others. They may burn sage or incense, light a candle, ring a bell, wash their hands, or mist themselves with a purifying spritzer, all with the intention of breaking the energetic connection between themselves and the client they just worked with. All of these symbolic gestures give the message to the healer's psyche to come back within itself and release the other with a blessing. Here is a silent prayer of release: *I acknowledge the importance of our connection, and it is now time to release _____ from my energy field with blessings upon his / her well-being.*

This practice could be helpful for you if you are unable to separate yourself from the pain that others are going through. Try using one of these techniques to intentionally break the energetic connection if, after talking to a friend going through a difficult time, you find yourself still carrying the weight of the conversation.

Fourth Chakra for the Spiritually Inclined

Just as your heart chakra is open to the depths of personal love, it is equally open to the heights of spiritual love. Spiritual love is honoring the spiritual essence behind the human mask in all beings. As you awaken to the spiritual love of your heart chakra, you relate to others with loving-kindness, compassion, and a deep acceptance. This allows others to feel safe to be themselves in your presence. You start seeing that all of life is woven together in a vast web of relationships—that we are all in this together—and you live your life accordingly.

The spiritual love of the fourth chakra is love as a state of being independent of the actions of others. The salutation *namaste*—of bringing your hands together at your heart while bowing slightly and acknowledging the divine spirit in others residing in their hearts—is an example of spiritual love, of loving the spiritual essence of all of creation.

Devotional practices of spiritual love from the heart chakra are joyous outpourings of the heart celebrating the love of the divine, such as Bhakti yoga and Sufi dancing. Devotion for spiritual masters whose guidance has led you to your spiritual source is another way to cultivate this higher octave of love.

Indiscriminate Spiritual Love

Indiscriminate spiritual love becomes an issue when you feel a spiritual heart chakra connection with another and try to make it personal in an inappropriate way. Fourth chakra love is beyond the personal chakras, and it is possible to have heart connections with many, many people; the heart is unlimited in its capacity to love. However, attempting to form a personal or romantic relationship with everyone you connect with at the higher level of your heart chakra would obviously be disastrous.

Learn to appreciate and value the rare heart chakra connections for what they are in and of themselves. The truth is that heart chakra friends are rare. We can talk about the universal quality of spiritual love, but how many people do we actually connect with at the heart level in a lifetime? "Because we feel this rare love for each other, it must mean we are supposed to be together," and so forth, is how the personal chakras want to get involved and weave their justifications into disastrous entanglements. This most often destroys what they already had and were attempting to get: soul love. Not body love, but spiritual love. If you already have that with a friend, treasure the rare gift for what it is before risking losing it by attempting to make the relationship romantic.

Fourth Chakra Difficulties and Solutions

You will experience increased joy from deeply loving and accepting others with an open heart chakra, but this is also where you must be open to experiencing the grief and sorrow that come from the loss of loved ones and broken relationships.

Attachment and Grief

Grief is the natural and healthy response to the loss of a loved one, particularly through death. Grief is caused by love and is healed by love. The function of grief is the honoring of the loss of a loved one, which after healing allows for an ongoing meaningful relationship with the departed in your psyche.

Just as the departed go through stages of transition in death, those grieving the loss also go through similar transitions. If you are closely connected to someone who has just died, your first few weeks will be as if you were in the transition states of dying yourself—time warps the ticking of the clock, so minutes can feel like days and days can feel like minutes. When you are not totally immobilized, you likely will find yourself meandering through your days, not sure how you got where you are or where you might be going.

It is important to first acknowledge the pain of the separation and the personal loss of a loved one. After a time, the grief moves to cherished memories of special times. Eventually grief transforms into a deep gratitude for the role the person played in your life and acceptance of their new role as part of your ascended family. This process is healthy and creates a healthy place within your psyche for your departed loved one.

When the natural emotion of grief (or any powerful emotion) is blocked and not allowed to be experienced, it doesn't go away; instead, it becomes stuck in the psyche.

Grief is as natural as death itself, and skill is required to avoid getting lost in your grieving heart. In *The Tibetan Book of Living and Dying*, Sogyal Rinpoche shares the Tibetan teachings on the role of those who have lost a loved one. Personal grief is natural and healthy and must be given its due, but the Tibetan teachings show how important it is to help loved ones navigate the transition states in between births, called *bardos*, with the intention of helping them toward a favorable rebirth. This is a healthy attitude that honors both your personal grief and the help you can provide for a friend with your prayers and intentions to help them navigate toward the light.

It is never too late to say the one thing you wanted to say but didn't get a chance. Grief is often attended with the feelings of having unfinished business with someone who has just died. These feelings of unfinished business are particularly poignant if you recently had an argument or difficulty of some kind with the person, but feelings of unfinished business are often there even if your relationship was in a good place at the time of the death. These are the voices of unfinished business: "There is just one thing I wanted to tell her before she died." "I didn't get a chance to apologize before he died." "I wasn't able to be there at the time of her death, and I feel terrible that she might feel I didn't care." "I just wish I had been able to be with him one last time, and now it's too late."

When the soul leaves the body, it is no longer subject to the restraints of space and time. The soul is free; distance and separation hinder it no longer. The dead are our nearest neighbors; they are all around us. Thinking of the eternal world where souls go after death as some distant place projects our limited perspective onto the unlimited realm of spirit. The eternal world of spirit is not so much a place, but rather is a different state of being. The spiritual essence of those who have died, being unbound by space and time, is here with us. You can sense their presence.

Time is not an arbiter in the timeless realm of death, and it is never too late to continue working on your relationship with someone who has died. The teachings suggest that the soul liberated from the body is seven times more clairvoyant than before and is receptive to even your silent messages and prayers.

Death and Choiceless Awareness

After awakening to your eternal spiritual nature, you realize that life and death are two sides of the same coin. You no longer are worried about death, realizing that no choice is involved in whether you will die or not. Then you live with choiceless awareness concerning death, knowing it is not about choice. By coming into a deep acceptance of this truth, you will be ready when your own death happens of its own accord.

It is considered one of the greatest blessings to die in the presence of someone aligned with the light of spirit, and it is helpful to remember this if you are called to be with someone who is dying. It is an incredible privilege and honor to be present at this sacred time of transition. By honoring the sacredness of the moment and with your highest intention set on seeing the soul ascend toward the spiritual light, you become like a beacon illuminating the way for the one dying.

Broken Heart

Life experiences that have a strong impact on the heart chakra also include the ending of a relationship, particularly when it is not initiated by you. These are the tough experiences in life that lead to a broken heart. Betrayals of the heart, such as getting cheated on in a relationship or a close friend breaking your trust, are also registered in your heart chakra, and until they are cleared, your heart can't remain open.

Getting back to an open heart will require forgiveness of the other if the transgression was on their part and self-forgiveness if it was you who was the betrayer. The first stage of forgiveness is rising up to be strong enough of character to accept the humanness of yourself and others. We all carry some of the darkness that comes from being in a human body, be it jealousy, lust, greed, envy, suspicion, resentment, a judgmental nature, anger, and on and on. With the heart chakra, there comes acceptance, and this ultimately has to include accepting the truth of these lower aspects of the human nature that everyone must wrestle with one way or another.

In an interesting twist on how we typically use affirmations, Marcus Aurelius, a Roman emperor and Stoic philosopher from the second century, suggests starting the day by affirming that you will encounter many of these lower aspects of human nature throughout the day so as to not be surprised or taken aback by such behavior: "Begin each day by telling yourself: Today I shall be meeting with interference, ingratitude, insolence, disloyalty, ill-will, and selfishness—all of them due to the offenders' ignorance of what is good or evil." [4]

This will help pull you out of yourself should you encounter this type of behavior and realize it is all about how you respond to it. You are going to encounter a considerable number of humans acting like humans that you won't be able to change, and knowing this frees you to go about your work of staying centered in the face of it.

This strength of character that is required to accept human frailties in yourself and others allows for the second stage of forgiveness: being willing to learn a lesson about yourself in the process. Strong character is required to be willing to look at the shadowy aspects of yourself that were revealed in the problem you are working on forgiving. "It takes two to tango" is the expression we use to imply that there is a lesson to learn in everything. It is the realization that you could have handled something better in the situation for which you want to forgive another.

This willingness to learn something about yourself even through difficulties with others helps you maintain an open heart—

---

4. Marcus Aurelius, *Meditations*, trans. Georg Long (167 CE; reprint, Enhanced Ebooks Publishing, 2012).

and the ability to grow and improve even through the painful challenges that do arise in relationships.

Guilt

Guilt and shame are often at the core of a blocked or restricted heart chakra and must be overcome in order to experience one's natural and healthy sexuality and loving nature. There is a healthy part of guilt that prods you to make amends and improve yourself, particularly when the guilt arises from pain you caused others. It is healthy if and only if the guilty feelings provoke changes in you for the better. However, unresolved guilt or shame that is just carried around endlessly shuts down your heart chakra.

Take Charge of Your Guilt Center

To take charge of your guilt center is to understand the value of guilt in your learning process. The healthy function of guilt is to sound an alarm from the moral compass of your Higher Self. The learning curve of life will present successes and failures at whatever you are trying to improve upon, and if you learn as much from every guilty mistake as you do from every success, there will never be ultimate failure—just another chance to improve.

Learn, Adjust, Atone

To form a healthy relationship with guilt, first ask yourself, "What can I learn from this?" Then make the adjustment, atone for your error in one way or another, and let go of the guilt. It has served a worthy purpose, and carrying it any further would be damaging. When, after making a mistake of one type or another, you find yourself saying, "I really learned something this time," this is actually only the first awareness of where learning needs to take place. The next time you face a similar situation, if you make the adjustments to avoid falling in the same chuckhole, then you can say learning has taken place.

Atone. Apologize to whomever you have hurt or offended. It takes largeness of character to acknowledge the pain you may have caused others, but it absolutely works to liberate yourself from the sentence of "guilty." When the judge in a courtroom pronounces someone guilty, a fine or some other type of sentence is then levied to even the score. Pay the fine and serve the time, and then your karma has been resolved and you are free. Score settled, move on.

Carrying guilt beyond its educative value is more than worthless; it is damaging. The best advice is to simply get over it, particularly when the guilty feelings are caused by not living up to your perception of other people's judgments of you. Only you are inside yourself; you are the only authority of your moral integrity. Others can't read your moral compass. Unless their judgment echoes your own Higher Self's judgment, it is worthless. Beyond youth, when moral training from parents and adults is necessary to learn to live with others, external standards aren't helpful.

Excessive moral training leads to a sense of guilt and shame over your humanness, restricting the flow of love from the diminished sense of worthiness and doubting how someone could fully love you. As you practice greater self-acceptance, you experience the redemptive, healing quality of love. The heart breaks and heals, breaks and heals, breaks and heals a thousand times in a life;

that is what it does. The redemptive quality of love is such that it heals old wounds completely—trusting in this begins the healing.

Shame and Vulnerability

Where guilt has a healthy function, shame has none. Guilt is associated with something you've done, but shame is attached to yourself, not just the behavior. Feelings of guilt can be levied by your Higher Self as part of your moral navigation, while shame always comes from your Lower Self and concerns some false measure of who you think you should be. For women, the false measure is often not living up to being a superwoman and showing up for everybody who needs them. For men, feelings of shame often stem from showing weakness in any way. These unrealistic standards are not being set by the Higher Self, but by the Lower Self's image of perfection.

Vulnerability

Courage is necessary only when we are vulnerable. The two go hand in hand: if we weren't vulnerable, we wouldn't need courage.

Accepting your human frailties that you have worked so hard to overcome can make you feel vulnerable. Showing your vulnerability at your power chakra (third chakra) is looked at as a sign of weakness to be avoided, lest someone take advantage of you, while revealing your vulnerability at your heart chakra is a sign of strength of your acceptance of even your human frailties and allows you to drop the armor protecting a false image of yourself. Dropping the armor is what opens the door to intimate heart connections, which is what your heart chakra seeks, and you move forward with your vulnerability rather than overcoming it.

Activities to
Empower Your Fourth Chakra

To bring more heart energy into your life, first off, don't wait for love. *To live the life you love, love the life you live.* This bumper-sticker type of wisdom has great merit in activating your heart chakra. To live more from the heart, bring the heart's joy into everyday living.

Your heart animates your life at all levels. Put your heart into all you do and your life will coalesce around this radiant source of energy. It's the difference between being wholehearted or half-hearted in what you are doing. To put your heart into something is to put your creative energy into bringing out the possibilities of life. Tease out the beauty of a meal you are creating, a person you are in conversation with, a project you are doing, or a lover you are caressing, and this will strengthen the manifesting energy of your heart field.

Practice self-love regularly by resting in your Higher Self, and radiate love, appreciation, gratitude, compassion, and forgiveness to your human self and all of its foibles.

Practice gratitude and thankfulness every day for all the loved ones in your life.

Practice loving-kindness toward yourself and others until it's no longer a practice but a way of being. Even when a relationship has run its course and must end, practicing loving-kindness by not saying unkind things to each other, or to others about each other, will make a difficult situation all the more bearable.

Additional Activities
to Enhance Your Fourth Chakra

Keep the heart and lungs pumping for increased circulation and a healthy heart chakra. This includes all aerobic activities, from physical exercise to dancing. Doing yoga postures that open your upper chest, such as bridge pose and camel pose, while breathing deep into the upper chest is excellent for your fourth chakra. Breathe with the rhythm of life pumping the vibration of love into every cell in your body.

Affirmations for Your Fourth Chakra

I am grateful for all the love that has been given to me, and I gladly share my love with others.

I accept the things and people in my life as they are.

My heart is full of the love of life, and I gladly share with others from this fullness.

In the center of my heart is goodness and light that no darkness can touch.

Love courses through every cell in my body with its healing energy.

Body Associations

The heart, lungs, esophagus, circulatory system, rib cage, breasts, arms, hands, and thymus gland are all associated with the heart chakra. Difficulties with any of these areas of the body signal a need to focus more on your heart chakra to help restore well-being.

Fourth Chakra Foods

The air element of your fourth chakra benefits from vegetables that grow in the air as well as from all green, high-in-chlorophyll vegetables. Broccoli, green cabbage, celery, cauliflower, kale, spinach, sprouts, salads, raw foods, green tea, chai, basil, sage, cilantro, and parsley all enhance your heart chakra. Foods prepared with love for you, such as birthday cakes, breakfast in bed, and special meals, though not necessarily nutritious, always bring a smile from your awakened heart chakra.

Fourth Chakra Gemstones

Emerald, rose quartz, aventurine, jade, malachite, peridot, and chrysocolla can all revitalize your heart chakra. You can hold a healing stone on your body where it needs attention; carry the stone with you or near you to enhance your environment and draw on its benefits.

Fourth Chakra Journaling

Now that you have read about your fourth chakra, this would be a good time to stop and contemplate the openness of your heart and record your insights in your journal. A person with an awakened heart chakra has compassionate acceptance of others and acts with loving-kindness in the world. Ask yourself if you have been accepting of those you love even though their views, opinions, and lifestyle choices may be different from yours. Ask yourself where you could practice greater loving-kindness in your dealings in the world. Record your insights.

CHAPTER 6

Fifth Chakra: Vishuddha

Location: Throat

Element: Ether, space

Symbol: A circle within a descending triangle within a larger circle with sixteen lotus petals

Color: Sky blue

Principles: Purification, communication

Key Benefits: The ability to know and speak your truth

Key Obstacles: Gullibility and lies, including the untruths we tell ourselves

Spiritual Qualities: Truth speakers and evolutionary agents for others

Type of Intelligence: Intuitive sudden knowing of truth

Your fifth chakra's placement at your throat shows its central role in expressing yourself and in all matters of communication. An awakened throat chakra gives you the ability to express your authentic truth while listening to others for the truth behind their words. As the bridge between your head and your heart, your throat chakra gives you the ability to speak your truth with love. An integrated fifth chakra comes from developing respect for what you uniquely have to offer in the grand scheme of things and an equal respect for the uniqueness of other people's perspectives.

If your throat chakra is underdeveloped, you will have difficulty expressing yourself, making meaningful communication a challenge. Being unclear of your own truth, you tend to give mixed messages with your vague and uncertain communications, making it difficult for others to get to know the real you. Speaking your truth and being honest with yourself is not easy with an underdeveloped fifth chakra, but it is the way to liberation.

The Sanskrit meaning of *vishuddha* is purification. Vishuddha requires a deep purification of body, mind, and consciousness to express your authentic truth. Vishuddha purifies the mind of its inconsistencies and unconscious patterns by seeing immediately the core essence of truth without attachment. As the first chakra above the heart, it is where you can cultivate detachment to see things just as they are, above sentiment, values, and opinions. Vishuddha provides insights born of the clarity of the truth of the moment.

It is this detachment that allows you to deal with the tough issues in life that do arise, like tragic losses and failures in your own life and the tragedies that beset others. With vishuddha, you look for the greater meaning of the experience within the bigger picture of life.

The element of the fifth chakra is ether, empty space—the same empty space that flows through all of creation. This awakens in you a vast, objective, and impartial nature, which can rise above all polarities within yourself, others, and the world. With an open vishuddha, you are able to transcend time, space, and logic to know something directly through the subtle etheric imprints recorded in all pervasive space and experienced as sudden insights.

The slicing discernment of the truth-seeking of vishuddha cuts through all of the unconscious ways you express yourself and use words indiscriminately. Awakening to your throat chakra, although it governs speech, doesn't necessarily make you more verbal. Chit-chat and idle gossip hold little interest for you in the light of the greater truth you seek. *Words are helpful, harmful, or useless*, and since you are extremely conscious of the energetic impact of all words, you are very discerning in what you say. When communicating, you don't respond immediately to everything that is spoken to you by others. You often wait for a moment to get a sense of what they are communicating beyond just the words.

Although some people do become less verbal as they become aware of their fifth chakra, this is radically different for an individual whose siddhi[5] from an awakened throat chakra is public speaking. If this is your creative gift of expression, then you are able to speak eloquently and articulately, and original insights seem to flow from you uninhibitedly.

Awakening to your fifth chakra inspires creative ways to express your innovative insights, such as poetry, writing, speaking, music, and painting, but creativity isn't limited to the fine arts. From using technology to reaching a student as a teacher, the innovative, fresh

---

5. *Siddhis* are special spiritual, supernatural, magical powers and abilities that can arise from spiritual awakening.

outpouring of creative insight is the measure of an awakened fifth chakra.

As the first of the upper three chakras, which are collective in nature, your fifth chakra awakens your interest in issues common to all of humanity, expanding your sense of connection to the great circle of life. You perceive the big picture of any situation, looking toward the future for possibilities and with an attitude of expectancy. The penetrating insights born from your fifth chakra are not simply perception or vision, but an active, creative process of looking for possibilities. Just as the mind anchored in the senses strives to reach the most accurate perception of reality, so the vishuddha level of intelligence aspires to encompass the greatest possibilities in any situation.

Authentic Truth

All matters of knowing and speaking your truth come from your throat chakra. To express your truth, you first have to know your truth. Those who have an integrated fifth chakra got there by valuing truth more than convention. They are speakers of truth and won't sell out to social convention when it compromises truth.

Awakening to your fifth chakra comes from trusting your authentic, direct perception of truth over and above all the conditioning you've received from others. From vishuddha, you move away from looking to others for truth toward inward, direct knowing and insight for verifying truth.

As vishuddha is the first of the upper chakras and is transcendent of the ego, awakening to your fifth chakra first requires questioning everything that you have been taught and conditioned to believe by your culture, in light of your own direct perception of the truth. It requires letting go of all remembered learning from the past to see things fresh in the moment. *Truth does not need to be remembered; it always freshly reveals itself.*

The freedom of the liberated perception of your fifth chakra is blocked by all of the conditioning and learning you have received from others. It is necessary to examine these stories and root out the false stories that you have carried about yourself and life that don't support the authentic truth of your being. Ask yourself where your self-image and view of life come from. Have you unquestioningly accepted the views of others as yours without examining them through your own direct experience? It takes courage to stand in your own truth.

How do you know if it is a false story you've been carrying about yourself? Your fifth chakra is of the element of space. When you examine a story or belief that you have been carrying, ask yourself, "Do I feel any constriction? Tightening? Limiting?" This is not the truth of spacious vishuddha. If you examine a story you've been carrying about yourself and you stay spacious and light throughout your investigation, keep the story. It is standing up to the litmus test of vishuddha. If you feel constriction, fear, or tightness, it is not your truth, and it is best to discard it. Why battle a false story in the first place?

Thoughts are energy and carry an emotional energetic frequency that can be felt. Some thoughts make you feel bad, and others make you feel open and expansive. Learn to distinguish between the two and free yourself from the disturbing thoughts. Just let them go.

Ask yourself, "What is the energetic price I pay to believe this thought or line of thinking?" When your body and emotions are uncomfortable and tight, ask yourself, "What am I thinking that is not based in truth and is causing this constriction?"

This allows you to fine-tune your inner work of knowing specifically which particular thoughts are leading to restriction in your energy field. Spacious awareness is the nature of vishuddha. Tune yourself to that frequency and then notice specifically which thoughts pull you out of that state and what type of mental activity allows you to stay in this spacious awareness.

"The mind is a wonderful servant but a terrible master." This familiar saying reveals the truth of the mind. Thoughts that arise from your thinking mind are divisive in nature. That is what the mind does. Your mind takes the immense whole of information coming in at any moment and analyzes, divides, and filters it into something manageable in the moment.

Quit the Habit of Thinking

To cultivate your ability to get the fresh insights that come from an awakened fifth chakra, quit the habit of thinking. Actually, you can't quit thinking. No one can. The mind generates thoughts—that is what it does all day long, nonstop. These uncalled-for thoughts are the mind's natural effervescence; like bubbles in champagne, they just arise uncalled for, and you can't use your mind to quiet the mind.

You can cultivate your ability to watch this phenomenon without attaching yourself to the never-ending parade of thoughts. Estimates are that perhaps up to 98 percent of the thoughts going through the mind are not adding anything to the moment other than maintaining its story. The mind is shameless in its insistence on going where it wants to go, and not necessarily where you want to go. But along with our petty thoughts, we also have more lofty, noble, and honorable thoughts that we feel good about having. As the saying goes, there is a saint and a sinner inside each of us. If the mind is a garden, some of the thoughts are certainly the beautiful flowers in human consciousness and some are the weeds. Which do you tend to in your mind's garden?

What you have to give is your attention; you do have a choice in how this currency is spent. What you pay attention to grows. Pay attention to the weeds and they will grow to dominate your consciousness. Water the flowers with your attention and they will grow to dominate the landscape of your mind.

The Urge for Freedom of Expression

Beyond a reactionary level of simply rebelling in the face of convention, your fifth chakra is the urge to be free to be your most authentic self. Rebelling against something is a reaction to it, and therefore you are still tied to it and not free. Thus there are two stages to this process: *fighting for your right to be free* and *expressing your right to be free*. During the first stage you need to prove your right to be free, and therefore you need someone or something to prove it to. So you attract some controlling, constraining person or situation into your life to break free of.

At a higher level, you simply express your right to be free. Other people's approval or disapproval doesn't weigh as heavily on your psyche, freeing you to express your authentic truth. The greatest freedom isn't freedom from others; it's the freedom from reaction to others. Shifting from a *freedom against* perspective to a

Freedom to

freedom to perspective liberates your fifth chakra to receive its innovative insights, bringing discovery into all aspects of life.

With an awakened fifth chakra, the inner chatter and self-conflict begin to quiet, giving you the ability to see things with absolute clarity. As your fifth chakra awakens, you see everything the mind and senses can gather within the bigger picture of the moment. This seeing from the whole rather than through a part is the basis of the insights and innovation that come from an awakened fifth chakra.

Detachment

Your fifth chakra awakens the spiritual quality of detachment that is necessary to see essential truth. Before you have awakened to the detached perspective of your fifth chakra, you are not able to see the suffering in the world without getting pulled into it. Without this spiritual quality of detachment, you would have to avoid seeing so much of the truth of life because it is just too painful. As you awaken to your fifth chakra, your ability to serve others and help in the world is greatly enhanced because you no longer need to shield yourself from truth or frame things in a certain way; you just see truth. This detachment allows you to stay in the clear Observer mode even while experiencing or witnessing emotionally trying experiences.

It takes detachment and strength of character to handle the piercing insights of vishuddha in the moment when you may be acting in some unconscious way. Your awakened vishuddha will let you know when you are not speaking your truth, and it takes brutal self-honesty to see beneath your illusions as to where you may be deceiving yourself.

Truth Seekers, Truth Speakers

People with an awakened throat chakra are often messengers and alarm clocks helping others wake up. You want to know people's direct experience of truth, not what they have read, heard, or been taught or how they think things should be. You are interested in your own direct experience of truth and won't settle for less than that from others. As you awaken to your fifth chakra, you help others question the false truths they have been carrying. Life coaches often have an awakened fifth chakra, and they instinctively find ways to help liberate others from limiting beliefs they have been carrying.

With experience at being an evolutionary agent in the lives of others, you grow to understand the delayed response you often get in response to your wake-up calls. People often don't like the alarm clock in the moment it wakes them from a deep sleep, and so it is with some of the messages that you have to share from an awakened fifth chakra. People tend to resist information outside of their existing beliefs, and you grow to realize it is necessary to let your messages germinate in the other person's psyche at their own pace. Be like the mail delivery person with your gifts of insight you offer: deliver the message and then let others decide how and when they will respond to it. With a balanced fifth chakra, you are beyond attempting to convince someone of your point of view, and you freely offer your insights without attachment as to how they are received.

With an awakened throat chakra, there will be times when some of the things you say, even in casual conversation, may have deep meaning and significance for others. You might not even realize that while giving an apparently random example of something you are discussing, the "random" story was exactly the experience of the person you are talking to, making the hair stand up on the back of their neck (throat chakra). These are fifth chakra surges of awareness lighting up the fifth chakra in others.

Truth without Heart

Truth without heart is often mean-spirited. Truth without the understanding and compassion for others that one develops from an integrated heart chakra leads to a verbally abusive personality.

Gossiping and expressing irritation about other people lacks heart. If you are working on eliminating negativity from your speech, you will find that your efforts are greatly enhanced not just by simply editing negative words out of your language, but by working on cultivating the soil from which words sprout, your fourth chakra.

It's not the words; it's the vibes. Words expressed through your fifth chakra are born of the soil of your fourth chakra. Words are initiated with your will in your third chakra, then pass through your heart chakra to be ultimately expressed through your fifth chakra. The chakra just beneath the chakra you are working with is its foundation. The strength and quality of your heart chakra absolutely determines the quality of the energy available to your fifth chakra. If you find yourself expressing more negativity about others than you wish, cultivate loving-kindness in your fourth chakra and the flower of your expression will change on its own.

When you find yourself being judgmental and opinionated about someone else, you are essentially saying, "If I were that person, I wouldn't live that way." The obvious fatal flaw in this type of thinking is that you are not that person. You do not have the same genetic make-up, family history, life experiences, and so forth of the other person. The teaching of "walk a mile in the other person's shoes before you judge them" speaks right to the point, as does the saying "If you knew the secret life of your enemy, they wouldn't be your enemy." [6]

The Vibration of Sound and the Fifth Chakra

Sound vibrations are registered in your throat chakra. Communication is highly influenced by tone—the same words can be said with different tones and give very different meanings. Musicians have forever utilized the effect that sound vibration has on consciousness to our great delight.

Cymatics is the study of the effect that sound vibration has on matter, typically demonstrated on the surface of a plate or membrane of some sort. A composite mixture of sand on the viewing plate can be seen responding to the influence of sound. The sand forms itself into specific unique patterns in response to various tones and sounds near it. These studies on sound waves made visible substantiate what we instinctively already know, tone matters.

The vibrational tone of your voice influences communication, and your tone delivers as much of your message as the words you use. When there is discordance and dissonance in the tone of your voice, others respond first to the energy, filtering the words of what you are saying through your tone.

Imagine you're having an argument with someone who says something unkind and then apologizes with the famous words

---

6. David Pond, *Astrology and Relationships* (St. Paul, MN: Llewellyn Publications, 2001).

"I'm sorry." You know in an instant if the words are being said from an open or closed heart by the tone, not just the words.

As you develop the listening skills of your fifth chakra, you become skilled at reading the tone, body language, gestures, and silent glances from others as part of their communication. You hear their words as part of the whole of their entire energy field, giving you added insights into the meaning behind their words.

When I was a young astrologer, an actress offered me a gift after her astrology session. She shared a lesson she learned in theater to not just speak from your throat but also to engage your diaphragm and deep belly by consciously being aware of them as you speak. This engages more of your total energetic being in the tone of your voice, and people will not only hear what you are saying but will also feel it deep in their being.

I found this lesson to be an invaluable fifth chakra lesson. I speak a deeper truth while engaging more of my chakras in what I'm saying, and I've grown to trust that the vibration of my voice will contribute to my message being understood by others. I've also grown to trust this when listening to others and knowing if what they are saying is just mental banter or a deeper truth.

Discovery without End

On the path of awakening to your Higher Self, there is no endpoint of ultimate awakening, as if once you get there, that's it. Get "there" and consciousness will continue to evolve and reinvent itself without end. Awakening to your fifth chakra stimulates the thrill of discovery of this eternally evolving consciousness, often giving you fresh insights and innovative ideas. The 1997 television commercial narrated by Richard Dreyfuss and promoted by Steve Jobs, the pioneering voice behind Apple Computer, said it well. In their "Think Different" campaign, they acknowledged and lifted up those who are often labeled as rebellious, crazy, or misfits. They applauded these individuals as the ones who think outside the box and, as a result, create change in our world.

Invite Novelty into Your Life

To keep the innovative quality of your fifth chakra sharp in your life, stay away from intuition-killing sameness. Too much routine and sameness in your life enforces expectations and dulls the need for intuition and discovery. New situations keep your attention sharp and require you to draw on your intuition and hunches to navigate unfamiliar terrain. Although your lower chakras are comforted by familiarity and life proceeding according to your expectations, too much of this is a killer for your intuition, as it sits idle, an unneeded resource.

Invite novelty into your life to strengthen your fifth chakra's fresh, in-the-now orientation. Our modern cities are rapidly stamping out novelty, with each city becoming much like every other city, with the same stores and much the same layout. Seek out the parts of town that have something unique to offer to feel the vitality of vishuddha. Shake up your routines for the weekend's entertainment and cultural exploration to activate your ability to get fresh insights and innovative ideas in your life.

Fifth Chakra
Difficulties and Solutions

Fifth chakra difficulties, whether from diminished or excessive expression, will make effective communication with others difficult.

We will cover difficulties with diminished expression first and then move on to excessive expression issues.

Diminished Expression of the Fifth Chakra

Doubt and negativity will hinder the development of your ability to offer the original insights that come from a balanced fifth chakra. With your continued allegiance to your Higher Self, seeking truth outweighs the negative hindrances from the lower chakras and doubt has less impact on your psyche. Purification occurs not only on the physical level but also on the level of the psyche and mind. All problems and unpleasant experiences that you have "swallowed" and suppressed during the course of your life continue to exist in the subconscious mind until they are faced and resolved with wisdom.

Difficulty expressing your truth is resolved when you eventually stand tall in your truth and give voice to your perspective in an empowering way. Speaking your heart's truth is healing, and often heals others. AA meetings are a good example of the healing benefits that come from sharing the unvarnished truth, both for those telling their truth and those listening.

Excessive Expression of the Fifth Chakra

When your throat chakra is over-emphasized or not integrated with your heart chakra, speaking up for yourself is never an issue, but problems may arise from the insensitive use of words.

If a person has awakened to the truth-seeing fifth chakra without first awakening to the heart chakra, they can be brutally insensitive. Truth without heart often hurts, and some people who are more allegiant to truth than heart can feel somehow noble in their piercing perceptions that cause pain, thinking, "Well, somebody had to tell them." Having an integrated fourth and fifth chakra gives you the ability to deliver even tough news in a way that can be well received by first making the other person feel safe before sharing the perspective that you think they need to hear.

Being overly opinionated is a clue to an unintegrated fifth chakra. Holding on to your truth as the only truth is just your personal opinion masquerading as truth and blocking the opportunity for discovery that comes from having a balanced throat chakra.

If you notice that this behavior of being overly opinionated is driving people away from you, the solution is not just to tame your tongue. It is even more important to cultivate the loving-kindness of your heart chakra, and you will find that the interfering behavior will dissipate on its own. You won't have to hold your tongue as you cultivate your sensitivity and care for others.

However, there are times when holding your tongue is exactly what needs to take place. If you find yourself being too talkative and need to give someone else a chance to express themselves, you could gently place your tongue on the roof of your mouth as a reminder to "hold your tongue."

Awakened Vishuddha and Sleeping Patterns

Your body needs food and sleep and your mind needs rest, but the creative spirit of an awakened fifth chakra operates unrestrained by the body's normal needs. What does empty space need to rejuvenate? Void of form and without need for physical energy yet filled with pure potentiality, the first stirrings of vishuddha awakening can at times be accompanied by major disruptions in one's normal eating and sleeping patterns.

Disrupted Sleep Issues

Disrupted sleeping patterns are familiar to many who struggle to stay asleep through the night. If this is familiar to you, why not try the old adage "If you can't beat them, join them," and embrace the sleeplessness in a healthy way. When struggling with sleep, the mind is terrible in the material it comes up with in the middle of the night. In these situations, you would likely prefer thinking about almost anything other than the mind's obsessions, and that is a good solution.

Why not schedule this time for studying the material that feeds your soul but is often difficult to find time for in a busy day? Reading an inspirational book is a much more delightful way to spend the time awake than struggling with sleep. As we age, we need less and less sleep. Teenagers go through phases requiring more than eight hours of sleep a night, but many people over fifty, and more women than men, are familiar with the "awake from 2:00 to 4:00 whether you want to be or not" syndrome.

This is a wonderful time to practice some of the meditation techniques that you might not have time for in a busy day. Try a meditation you can do lying on your back in a sleeping position. Following your breath and relaxing all tension in your body is excellent for getting the rest your body needs while also calming your mind.

There are times when you might as well get up, have a cup of tea, and putter around instead of trying to calm your energy and get back to sleep. After an hour or two, you can go back to bed and enjoy deep, restful sleep until you wake up and start your day.

As you let go of your resistance based on an earlier construct of your circuitry and how much sleep you think you need, you begin to discover that you have plenty of energy throughout the day. If you can allow for a catnap or short snooze sometime during the day, you will get your energy right back. A rigid adherence to trying to control energy that can't be controlled is exhausting. It's tough work to get that wave to quiet down!

Your sleeping environment has an impact on how restfully you sleep. It is wise to have your sleeping environment free of work projects, computers, clutter, and incomplete projects, which capture your psyche's attention even as your senses shut down. Light shining anywhere on the body is registered in the pineal gland, which modulates melatonin and sleep. Even if you wear a sleeping mask or have your head under the covers, if light is shining anywhere on the body, it will register with the pineal gland and interfere with its natural production of sleep-regulating melatonin.

Activities to
Empower Your Fifth Chakra

Awakening to your fifth chakra allows you to be a clear channel of truth and insight. Rumi has a theory that we are like hollow bamboo flutes and that sometimes some good music comes through. Allow the music of your being to play through you. There is something your soul came here to do in this life; pray that you become aligned with it and then surrender to what plays through the hollow flute of your being.

For astrologers, tarot card readers, energy intuitives, and others actively using their intuition in their work with others, vishuddha is all-important. Counselors, life coaches, healers, teachers, team leaders in business, and musicians tuning in to the group mind of the audience all benefit from the direct insight of vishuddha.

To keep your ability to express truth in the moment sharp, stay away from rote answers to questions and overly rehearsed teaching; these are from memory and mask intuition. Challenge yourself to tell the story fresh each time, whether it be a tarot card reading, an interpretation of an astrological pattern in someone's chart, or the way you are experiencing an energy healing exchange. Let it be fresh and expressed in a spontaneous way in the moment, and vishuddha will come into play.

It's not uncommon for me to see this principle in action in my astrology readings with clients. As we get going, I might spontaneously make up a scenario to describe what I'm seeing astrologically, such as, "It's as if you bought a blue jacket yesterday and feel like taking it back for a green one today." Not always but often enough to catch my attention, the response might be, "That is just what happened yesterday." Did the information come to me as if I heard it? No, not at all. I had no inkling of that story being exactly what my client went through. The story arose spontaneously in me, not to me, as if from the client but within myself.

This is how expressing intuition typically works for me. It arises spontaneously and is not something I first think and then repeat.

Looking for Something Missing

Your awakened fifth chakra can help you find missing objects. "You know where you are. Reveal yourself." Hold that intention and then go about your day. Intuitive guidance doesn't necessarily come as a mental image of seeing the missing keys and where they are. It most often operates by getting distracted by a towel on the floor that needs to be taken into the laundry room and there are your keys! Something led to your finding your keys beyond your willful attempts. It just happens.

Now Streaming

As you become skilled at staying in the present moment, which is where truth always reveals itself, you never feel a need to leave this moment to find a better moment. *You don't leave the now to get in touch with a better now; you bring the now with you.* By staying in the present moment, the world is no longer seen as problematic. You can stay in the aliveness of the moment and observe *Leela*, the play of divine consciousness, God's play of ever-changing phenomena. Let the forms come and go as they do.

Additional Activities to Enhance Your Fifth Chakra

Yoga Postures

Shoulder stand, camel pose, lion pose, and neck rolls all facilitate the flow of energy to your fifth chakra. You could silently chant the fifth chakra's seed tone, *Ham* (pronounced "hum"), during your postures to further enhance its opening.

Fifth Chakra Breathing

Contract the base of your throat and make the inbreath vibrate at the throat chakra so you can hear the sound of inrushing wind. Focus on your throat and the color sky blue as you are breathing to help activate your fifth chakra.

Affirmations for Your Fifth Chakra

I am open, honest, and clear in my communications with others.

I listen to others for the meaning behind their words.

I am free to be my most authentic self and honor the authentic self in others.

I gladly offer my unique creative talents to the world.

I begin this day with an open heart and open mind.

May I be fully absorbed in life more than in my thoughts about my life.

May I deeply listen and feel what others are saying more than thinking about what is being said.

I embrace this day.

Body Associations

The thyroid gland, throat, ears, mouth, teeth, jaw, neck, shoulders, and lymph glands are all associated with the fifth chakra. Difficulties with any of these areas of your body indicate a fifth chakra imbalance.

Fifth Chakra Foods

Blue foods and foods and beverages that detoxify the system and feed your thyroid all help fortify your throat chakra. Sea vegetables, soups, fish oil, ginseng, tree-ripened fruits, lemon and lime in water, fruit juices, herbal teas, slippery elm tea, borage flowers, and Echinacea all enhance your throat chakra. Good choices for recreational eating include ethnic foods that help you break out of routines and unify you with other cultures.

Fifth Chakra Journaling

After reading about your fifth chakra, stop and contemplate your associations with truth. Have you received insights from your Higher Self as to how you can be more effective at speaking your truth? Record your insights in your journal. In your communications with others, have you been listening with the intention of understanding the meaning beyond their words, or have you been filled with your own thoughts as others are speaking? Record your insights as to how you can improve your listening skills.

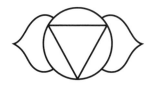

CHAPTER 7

Sixth Chakra: Ajna

Location: Center of brow

Element: Light

Symbol: A downward-pointing triangle within a circle and two lotus blossoms

Principle: Your spiritual eye

Key Benefits: Vision and the seat of awareness, the Observer

Key Obstacles: Illusions, escapism, fantasy

Spiritual Qualities: Access to inner guidance and spiritual wisdom

Type of Intelligence: Visionary

An awakened sixth chakra opens the door to all the wonders of the spiritual and psychic realm. Abiding in its awareness brings peace to your psyche and soothes your soul as you observe the outer theater of life from your seat in your inner awareness. As the seat of your Observer within, *ajna* gives you an expanded perspective, an inner seeing beyond what your senses are providing. The introspection necessary for inner vision magnetizes your spiritual eye by withdrawing attention from the sensory and outer world and focusing it on the source from where attention comes.

The Sanskrit meaning for ajna is "command," as in "to summon." To awaken ajna, it is necessary to direct your attention from the outer vision of your two eyes to the inner vision of your third eye. Awakening to ajna's inner vision gives you the ability to sense the workings of a greater intelligence and see patterns in this larger order. Its awakening may make you appear nearly psychic to others, while you are simply seeing the larger order, the bigger picture and its interconnections.

Light, vision, inspiration, inner guidance, and the psychic skills of the sixth chakra all sound so wonderful, but until you are skilled with spiritual vision, this opening is as much trouble as good! Your sixth chakra awakens the magic carpet of imagination, and its range of possible expressions can lead to inspiration for the skillful; but for the unskillful, escapism, crippling fear, and disassociation from reality can manifest. Just as we say the mind is a wonderful servant but a terrible master, the same could be said of your imagination, the vehicle of your sixth chakra.

Being skilled with the sixth chakra can lead to abilities with telepathy, astral projection, remote viewing, clairvoyance, seeing into the past and future, bliss from resting in pure awareness, rapport with other levels of intelligence, plant and animal communication, and communion with fairies, spirit guides, angels, Buddha, and Christ universal consciousness.

However, if you are untrained and unskilled, wandering into the astral plane of the collective imaginary realm can lead to illusions of all sorts, including sexual fantasies, escapism, fears that are simply made up, avoidance, deception (with self or others), disillusionment that invariably follows illusions, the terror of nightmares, feeling vulnerable to entities outside of your control, and savior-victim scenarios. Yes, this psychic realm is definitely as much trouble as good until you become skilled at navigating the magic carpet of where your capacity for imagination / vision can take you.

The light of your spiritual eye at the forehead is most often masked over by mental activity and undirected imaginary wanderings. With training in meditation, your spiritual eye can lead you safely into all spiritual and psychic activities, and it all begins with finding your way to the detached Observer within.

The Observer Is the Key to Awareness

The purest aspect of your sixth chakra in its receptive mode is the Observer level of consciousness within you, where you are simply aware of being aware. The Observer is the place within you that can observe the self even while the self is in action. "In the world but not of the world" points to this Observer in you, aware even of your thoughts and emotions while they are occurring.

Observing the experience you are involved in creates a little space between you and what you are observing. As your identity shifts to the Observer, you become aware of its unchanging nature witnessing the ever-changing reality before you.

This is the key to a great world of freedom—freeing you from the anxiety of trying to direct and make sense of the ever-changing phenomenal levels of reality. You learn to cultivate this vantage point of just "seeing" as the still point among the chaos.

If you master this level of pure Witness consciousness, you gain the ability to see things as they are without judgment, opinion, or attitude; you simply observe.

"To see things as they are without judgment" would be a pretty fair description of enlightenment on most spiritual paths. Although this is easy enough to say, it is seemingly impossible not to add your storyline to what you are observing, with judgments and opinions from the lower chakras coloring this pure perception of the Observer. Your Observer sees things just as they are from a larger perspective transcendent of thoughts and sensory information.

When your lower chakras are influencing your sixth chakra, they distort your vision and your ability to simply see by deflecting your vision to meet the needs of the interfering ego. To rise above this interfering chatter is somewhat easy for most of us to do in nature, where we can enjoy a walk in the park while simply seeing and observing the natural beauty and not constantly having an opinion about whether the trees are too tall or too short. Wouldn't it be great to have that same clarity with others, the world around you, and even yourself?

The Observer is the key. Without awareness of this witnessing part of your consciousness, you stay immersed in the ever-changing phenomenal world of the senses and thoughts. With the awakening of ajna and the vantage point of the Observer, you begin to become aware of the unchangeable nature of awareness itself. The place within you that is observing, witnessing, and aware is unchanging. Your awareness is not going through the ups and downs of your life; it is simply observing without reaction, simply being aware.

The spiritual eye of your sixth chakra is the door to another level of intelligence beyond that which the mind can reach, coexisting with the sensory world yet of another order of reality. You can't use your mind to get to the transcendent level of intelligence no matter how smart you are, because it is not in the realm of the mind. Spiritual awareness is not within your mind; *your mind is within your awareness.*

Meditation and mindfulness practices train your consciousness not to listen to the forever-yammering voices in your head but just to watch their exceedingly temporary nature. As you learn to rest in the pure awareness of the Observer level of consciousness, this becomes a resource within that you learn to access as your home base. Look for simple meditation and visualization exercises later in this chapter to help you get and stay there throughout the day.

If you are drawn to psychic phenomena and you first connect with the still, quiet perspective of the Observer level of your Higher Self, you will then be safe to explore the many magical dimensions of the astral realm. Touch base with your center first and ask for the guidance from your Higher Self that is helpful, loving, and lifting, and then you can trust that your wanderings in the astral realm will be sanctioned by your Higher Self.

As the seat of your attention stays firmly rooted in the perspective of your Observer, the ease of life from this perspective simply becomes preferred over wrestling with reality at the ego perspective. It's not that situations don't pull you out of this state, but their attraction diminishes as you learn to rest more and more in conscious awareness. You become aware of the energetic expense of the reactionary state of consciousness and simply choose not to get sucked into it.

You could hear news on the television that provokes an angry reaction within you and then start in on your own rant over the ranting you are hearing on the news. By staying in awareness, you immediately notice the tightening of your energy field following this reaction and choose to keep your attention with your awareness rather than your reaction, and the constriction relaxes. As was said in the introduction, you can't change the world, but you can change your reaction to it.

It Is Not *Just* Your Imagination, It *Is* Your Imagination!

Everyone has imagination. Imagination, when skillfully directed, can be a doorway to creative inspiration filling you with energy, or it can be unskillfully wasted through idle fantasy and escapism. Worse yet, imagination can lead to crippling, debilitating imagined fears. Those who are susceptible to imagined fears are vulnerable to the fear-making machine of the news media and those who manipulate through fear. Imagined fear and creative vision are made of the same imaginary stuff; one constricts and disempowers you, while the other fills you with rejuvenated inspiration.

Fear is so dominant in the collective astral field that you have to stay vigilant and compensate for this dominant collective influence. It is not that you have all this fear, but the field of the collective image bank of humanity has a crust of fear around the inspirational light at its core.

Your same imagination that can make up incredibly creative fear stories of "what if?" can instead be directed in soul-enriching directions that would be inspiring and empowering.

Although subtle and entirely inward, your ajna center is transpersonal in nature; thus, you access not only your images but also the archetypal, collective images of humanity. The astral plane is filled with as much garbage and goop as it is with pure inspiration. Left untended, your imagination becomes influenced by the ego, sinking downward into the muck of desires, fears, and escapist fantasies. Turn the lotus flower of your sixth chakra around, upward toward the light, and you can pull out of the muck.

Take responsibility for your access to this magical kingdom of inspiration and vision by staying in awareness of what you are imagining and its energetic effect on you. Learn to put down an imaginary fear as easily as you put down a bad book and reach for something more uplifting and enchanting.

Your Imagination and Fear Mongers

Terrorists are an extreme example of those who use fear to control people, while less-than-scrupulous leaders have long used fear to assert control. Manipulating people with fear can win their obedience but never their hearts. Hearts are won by the leaders who speak for the common vision of enhancing the quality of people's lives. Metaphysically, we know that whatever tests are showing up collectively are most assuredly happening on the individual level as well. Where are you allowing fear mongers to terrorize your heart, coercing you to make choices from the fear of "what if?" rather than living your life from your truth and your heart?

When my sons were first driving, I would at times find myself dwelling on my concern for their safety, worrying about this, that, or the other thing. My wife would counsel me at such times, offering her advice to "send angels instead." I like to believe that this may have helped them, but at a minimum, following her sage advice sure helped my psyche! It simply felt a whole lot better to be sending my sons positive, supportive images as opposed to wrapping them in my imagined fears.

As you work with developing your imagination/vision chakra, ask yourself if you are being responsible about the quality of your imagination and its energetic impact on others. Are you wrapping those you care about in your fear, or are you empowering them with your faith? Or, more simply, are you sending those you care about your positive or your negative energy? Which would be more helpful? Which would you rather receive from others?

Dreams

Along with your fantasies in your waking life, your sixth chakra governs your sleeping dreams. There are three main levels of dreaming.

Unfinished Business Dreams

This is the material of the day that passes through your conscious awareness and then resurfaces in dreams. People you saw or television shows you watched can trigger these dreams. Children's nightmare monsters often come from a scary image they saw in the media working their way into the dream realm.

At a deeper level, these dreams can bring up material from the subconscious, which is often something you are in denial of and do not want to look at. They can reveal buried material that has been pushed down, and these nightmarish dreams are often uncomfortable. They provide a window into something you probably haven't wanted to look at, and they give you the opportunity to experience some shadowy aspect of your character that needs to be brought into conscious awareness. It is useful to consider that each of the characters in your dream is acting out unclaimed aspects of yourself being projected onto the dream characters.

Conscious Dreaming

These dreams can occur when you are preparing for something important that you are doing in your waking life. They are essentially a dress rehearsal in the dream state. After these dreams, you may feel as tired as if you had been working all night, and energetically you have been.

Superconscious Dreams

These are the special dreams where you realize that you are aware that you are dreaming while in the dream. It is valuable to write down these dreams, as they often carry guidance from your Higher Self.

Dreams are a valuable resource of information about yourself that you would otherwise not have access to in your waking life. Keeping a dream journal is the surest way to get the fullest impact from your dreams. Tell yourself just before falling asleep that you intend to remember your dreams, and affirm your intention to write them in your journal.

Even vivid, meaningful dreams disappear and become inaccessible just moments after opening your eyes. A valuable technique for remembering your dreams is to not open your eyes when you first wake up and to tell yourself how you will write about the dream before you do. With your eyes still closed, remember the dream as if you were going to write it down in detail. This rehearsal in your mind makes it much easier to recount the dream as you open your eyes and begin to record it in your journal, which ideally you keep by your bed with a pen.

One of the benefits of a dream journal is in the encoding of the dream in and of itself. Simply writing the story and contemplating the images will give you valuable intuitive insights from your own Higher Self. Too much analyzing of your dream material robs it of its symbolic meaning, which your intuition gets guidance from but your analytical mind will miss.

Angels, Guides, and Spirit Buddies

Animism is the belief that all of creation has an animating spirit that should be respected. The unseen realm of spirit is of the sixth chakra. Native American traditions are rich with these teachings and have developed rituals for connecting with the unseen world of spirit. The Onondaga tribe in upstate New York is one such example in the way they conduct an opening ceremony of an important event. The leader of the ceremony silently sends greetings to and thanks for the people at the ceremony: "To all that is seen and unseen, it is named, greeted and given thanks. To Mother Earth and Father Sky, to the spirit of water, air, plants, animals, stones, the elements, the directions, to our teachers who have shown us the way and for all the gifts of creation and all the love around. And for all that is forgotten, we remember with our words." With this ceremony of uniting all minds with all of creation, they begin the event.[7]

---

7. Huston Smith, *And Live Rejoicing: Chapters from a Charmed Life* (Novato, CA: New World Library, 2012), pp. 137–139.

When my wife and I visited Findhorn, the garden community in Scotland, we noticed that group activities were initiated by an attunement prayer to what was referred to as the "Findhorn Angel." After a few days of getting to know the leaders of the community, I asked more about this and was told that the Findhorn Angel was a composite energy of all those who believed and supported the spirit of Findhorn. Members who assembled for an activity, like a garden project or the preparation of a meal, would all attune to this animating spiritual force together and then set about manifesting their vision with inspired assistance.

No decisions were made in Findhorn without 100 percent agreement among the involved members. This called for a coalescence of the group mind—surrendering to the guiding spirit of Findhorn to make the best decision for the good of the community.

I have incorporated this practice into my life by attuning to the attending spirits of our garden before starting garden projects. With a silent prayer, I acknowledge the presence of the presiding spirits of the garden and let them know I come as an ally to serve. My lighthearted way of aligning with these spirits is to first acknowledge their presence and then announce, "I'm the mobile unit here. What can I do to help?" Then I go about doing what I'm inspired to do after that invocation.

All those who have experience with angels agree on the point of how valuable it is to invite their assistance into your life to receive their assistance. I'm sure we all get some higher assistance by sheer grace, unasked-for cosmic interventions that just show up as special moments when certain disaster is at hand and is somehow avoided. "I thanked my guardian angel that time," someone might say of these rare moments of unforeseen magical intervention.

These acts of grace affirm that something is there to help, but to gain this assistance in your life on a more regular basis, you must ask for angelic help. "Ask, and it shall be given you; seek, and ye shall find; knock, and it shall be opened unto you." [8]

I have always been fascinated and rather enchanted by the concept of guardian angels and spirit guides. I've had enough experiences with divine intervention magically pulling me out of harm's way that I've become quite comfortable simply believing in their existence and benefit in my life. There was a time early in my astrology career when I was counseling a client as to how to deal with a particular transit going on in her chart and I found myself advising her to contact her guardian angels. As I said the words, I immediately heard my Higher Self as a voice in my head mocking me: "Oh, so now you are an authority on angels too?"

I realized that I had to either quit talking as an authority about something I knew very little about or earn the right by doing some research into the topic. Not being able to discount my experiences with divine intervention, I chose to delve in and read all that I could from multiple sources. After this study, I apparently satisfied my Higher Self in that it no longer intervened when I spoke of guardian angels to others. I was also impressed with how consistent the advice was from culture to culture: to enhance your openness to angelic assistance, it is of prime importance to invite and welcome angels into your life.

I saw this principle in action firsthand during a time of family crisis. I was teaching classes out of town when a record rainfall

---

8. The Bible, Matthew 7:7 (King James Version).

back home created a flood that engulfed the first floor of our house. Our small garden pond swelled to such a degree that goldfish could be seen swimming in the garage. Fire trucks arrived and attempted to pump the water off the property to no avail. My wife and children were forced to move upstairs, and all the drains were backed up for a week, meaning no laundry, flushable toilets, and so on. By the time I got back, they had become miserable dealing with this unhealthy situation.

Feeling the severity of their anguish, I furiously set about digging trenches to get the water moving and using a plunger on the drain in the basement shower, the low point in the house. After several attempts at plunging as long and hard as I could until I was fatigued, I cried out in futility, "Come on, angels! My family needs help. If you are there, please help me now." And with the next push, the drain opened. In stunned relief, I watched the water rush down the drain and found myself jokingly asking, "What, you guys help with plumbing too?" Apparently they do!

One caution about hanging out with spirit buddies, including angels, is that they don't need rest or sleep—but you do! To maintain a healthy life, it is necessary to make a few demands, or at least requests, of the spirit world, such as when you need sleep and rest. This you have to take responsibility for; you are the one in a body, and you need to know what your needs are for a healthy personal life so you can be of service. You can communicate your needs for healthy boundaries silently. Your spirit buddies will hear them and honor your requests. But don't expect your spirit allies to know your limits and needs for maintaining a healthy body; they don't know, but you must.

The Pineal Gland
and Your Sixth Chakra

The pineal gland, which is associated with your sixth chakra, sits between the two hemispheres of the brain and gathers information from both. The receptive and active energy channels of *ida* and *pingala*[9] merge here, and your spiritual eye synthesizes this information with awareness of the larger context of the subtle planes and intuitively "sees."

The pineal gland is a small pinecone-shaped endocrine gland. Its main function in the body is to produce melatonin, a derivative of the hormone serotonin, which affects sleep patterns. The pineal gland is located near the center of the brain between the two hemispheres, tucked in a groove where the two halves join. Unlike the rest of the brain, it is outside the blood-brain barrier and circulates more blood than any organ other than the kidneys.

There is considerable debate among authorities on whether the pineal or the pituitary gland is associated with the sixth chakra. That the pituitary gland is located lower in the brain and a bit more forward than the pineal gland lends support to the pituitary gland's association with the sixth chakra. However, the light-transducing function of the photosensitive pineal gland and its responses to light, the element of the sixth chakra, supports its connection to the spiritual eye. Mystical art has often used the pinecone as the symbol of the awakened third eye. It could be that since both the pineal and the pituitary gland are situated near the

---

9. Along with the central energy channel, *sushumna*, there are two subtle currents, *ida* and *pingala*, that begin at your first chakra, weaving through the ascending chakras and reuniting at your sixth chakra. Ida is the receptive yin channel and pingala is the active yang channel.

sixth chakra, they both are of the sixth chakra, and the seventh chakra is transcendent to both. The pineal gland converts light energy into an electrochemical impulse, stimulating the hypothalamus, which directs the pituitary gland as the master gland to secrete the right hormones throughout the body to achieve a healthy balance.

Meditation

All meditation and visualization activities exercise your sixth chakra. Meditation is a direct experience of the spiritual reality and creates cohesiveness in the brain like no other activity. A regular meditation practice synchronizes the brain, enhancing all intellectual, creative, and integrative brain functioning as well as providing spiritual insights.

It is interesting that the peace and tranquility we seek from meditation is always there when we turn to it! The more regularly you meditate, the more this practice makes permanent changes in your brain functioning, bringing the coherence (an experience of being co-here) of meditation into all aspects of life. Lifetime meditators have a calm about them that cannot be ruffled.

When our children were teenagers, I noticed an interesting pattern. I had been a meditator for most of my adult life, and although I was not always disciplined, after periods of neglect I would eventually return to my meditation practice. I began to notice that when there were major cycles of chaos with our sons, like fights at school, first car accidents, difficulties with teachers, and so forth, they often occurred when I wasn't meditating.

It struck me that there was no center in the family storm, and I would commit to getting back to my practice of getting in touch with my center. I wouldn't meditate about my children—they were already in my heart. I would just return to my own center, and it always seemed to help bring a calm to the family as well.

Tune Your Instrument

Imagine a great musician running late to get to his performance. As he gets to the theater, the audience has already assembled and is anxiously waiting. He can feel their expectation and readiness for him to come on stage and begin. But while unpacking his instrument, he notices it is badly out of tune. What is he to do? Rush onto the stage to satisfy their impatience and play disappointing music from an untuned instrument? Or take the time to tune his instrument and then play?

It seems silly to even imagine playing an instrument before tuning it, but how often do we begin our day without the attunement of the instrument of our being that meditation brings?

Practice
. . . .
Chakra Tune-Up Meditation

Sit in a comfortable posture with the spine straight. Practice deep breathing for a few minutes to calm your mind. On a slow, deep inbreath, picture energy coming up through the earth and your tailbone, up your spine, and out the top of your head. Next, on a slow exhalation, imagine energy flowing into your crown, down through your spine, and into the earth. You can let go of your attention on the breath now and rest in a comfortable breathing pattern.

Now focus on each of your chakras one by one, from your first chakra to your seventh chakra, spending time with each one until you get its message of what it needs to be brought into balance.

First focus on and contemplate your first chakra at the base of your spine, and breathe in the color red. Your first chakra is directly connected to your body, so check in with your body and ask how it is doing. Ask yourself what you have been doing lately to take care of your body with diet or exercise. Ask your body how it would like to be cared for, and listen for its response. Feel gratitude for having a body to experience life. Feel your connection to the earth itself, as your first chakra is your root, anchoring you to your body and drawing energy from the earth. Feel the security of knowing that life is living you as much as you are living life.

Next focus on and contemplate your second chakra, located just above your pubic ridge, and breathe in the color orange. This chakra activates your ability to enjoy and take delight in life and animates much of your emotional body. Ask yourself what you have been doing lately to enjoy and cultivate beauty in your life. Have you been denying this part of your character, leading to a lack of joy in your life, or have you focused too much on indulging in pleasure? Note what arises from your Higher Self in response to your contemplations of what your second chakra calls for to be brought into balance. Where is it that you can cultivate enjoyment and creativity and bring greater beauty into your life? Sit with these questions until you get the guidance from your Higher Self.

Next focus on and contemplate your third chakra, which is just above your navel, and breathe in the color yellow. This is your power and will center. Contemplate how you been have using your power and will lately. Are you making progress on something that you would like to achieve? Have you been practicing self-discipline, or have you been spinning your wheels, mired, with no direction? Have you been overly aggressive and assertive to the detriment of others, feeling powerless and blocked, or have you been balanced in your use of power? Ask yourself what you can do to demonstrate greater self-control to accomplish some task or project, and sit with this question until you get guidance from your Higher Self.

Now focus on your fourth chakra, at the center of your chest, and breathe in the color green. Contemplate your heart. Have you been practicing loving-kindness toward yourself and others, or has your heart felt heavy and closed? Who do you count in your heart circle, and can you feel your love and appreciation for heart connections in your life? Where has compassion touched you recently? Ask your Higher Self what it is that your heart needs to be cared for. Sit with these contemplations and note what naturally arises in your psyche in response.

Next bring your attention to your fifth chakra, at your throat, and breathe in the color sky blue. Contemplate how you have been expressing your truth lately. Have you been speaking from your heart? Have you been willing to give voice to your personal truth? Have you been willing to be a voice for others to wake up to their truth? Have you been acting on your intuitive flashes that arise in the moment, or have you ignored that inner knowing and then wished you hadn't? Contemplate these questions on your associations with truth, and note what arises in your psyche from your Higher Self in response.

Now bring your attention to your sixth chakra, at your brow between your eyes, while breathing in the color indigo blue. Contemplate how you have been engaging your imagination and the urge to transcend the everyday world. Have you been directing your imagination toward that which inspires you or that which depletes you? Have you been paying attention to where your imagination travels, or have you been letting it wander aimlessly? What have you been doing to tune your psychic antenna to the higher realms of inspiration? What does your sixth chakra call for to bring it into a healthy balance? Contemplate your relationship to your inner vision, and note what naturally arises from your Higher Self in response.

Now bring your attention to your seventh chakra, at the crown of your head, and breathe in the color violet or clear white light. Have you pulled your attention out of worldly considerations and connected with your spiritual source lately? Have you been surrendering to the empowerment of your soul urge and following it without question? Have you been lost in what you are aware of, or have you been aligning with the source of awareness? Have you connected to this unchanging, non-aging source of your awareness, transcending any sense of separateness from your spiritual essence? Listen to your Higher Self's response to your contemplations of your crown chakra on how you can be more open to your connection to the spiritual source.

After you complete these contemplations with each of your chakras, rest in quiet awareness, with gratitude and conviction to follow any guidance you received during your meditation. This is an excellent time to record your insights in your chakra journal.

. . . .

Sixth Chakra Difficulties and Solutions

Illusions are the chief obstacles of the sixth chakra. The spiritual resource of vision and imagination when ungrounded leads to illusions of all sorts. These can range from imagining potential that just isn't there in a relationship or a business, to all forms of the denial of truth being masked as "just being positive," to the illusion of being separate from the source of all of creation. All manifestations of illusion invariably lead to disillusionment, as the fantasy soap bubble of illusion eventually pops, and the pain of the broken dream follows. The good news is that after the bubble has burst, clarity returns and you again have the opportunity to use your vision in a healthier way, grounded in reality.

Inspiration Constipation

If you feel a lack of the inspiration that comes from an open sixth chakra, perhaps you are suffering from inspiration constipation—too many unacted-upon inspirations backing up your system. To capture more inspiration in your life, develop the courage and the commitment to follow through on the inspirational ideas that do come. When you feel some inspiration, follow through on it and you will develop greater trust with the source of inspiration.

Imagine an angel of inspiration whose role it is to dispense the inspirational nuggets that lift humanity's spirit upward. If such an angel were to exist, to whom might we expect this angel to give the juicer nuggets of inspiration? Someone who is likely to follow through on the vision or someone who rarely acts on the offered inspiration? Act with the attitude of "if I get the assignment, I will take the first steps to follow through on it." If you are inspired to help alleviate world hunger, vow to at least take a can of food to the food bank that day. If you are inspired to write a song, a play, or a book, vow to get at least one line written today. This relieves the inspiration constipation and develops greater trust with these agents of your Higher Self.

Activities to Empower Your Sixth Chakra

Meditation and visualization exercises in all of their many forms are the key to strengthening your spiritual eye. The following are some examples of methods for utilizing and enhancing your skill at navigating the subtle realms.

Exercise
. . . .
Kriya Yoga Meditation

This meditation was inspired by the Kriya Yoga practice taught by Paramahansa Yogananda in *The Art of Super Realization* and adapted to our work with the chakras. Yogananda called meditation "practice in the presence of

God," and that is the attitude and intention we approach
our meditation with.

First do a few stretches with deep breathing, and get
the prana circulating in the spine. After enlivening your
spine with a few stretches, sit with your spine erect and
straight in your most comfortable position for meditation.

Energy activation: On the inbreath, hold your mouth
lightly open, with your lips in a small "O," breathing in the
sound of your breath's wind all the way down to the base
of your spine.

Root lock: Practice the root lock as your breath gets to
the base of your spine by tightening the sphincter muscle
at its base. Focus your attention on your first chakra, and
feel grounded and centered in your body.

After a few first chakra breaths, on the next inbreath,
focus your attention on the energy rising in the sushumna
channel from your first chakra to your second chakra.
Apply the root lock, hold your breath for a moment, and
focus your attention as if you were looking out at life
through your second chakra. Orange is the color associated with the second chakra, but what color do you see or
sense through your second chakra today? As you breathe
out, picture yourself breathing out through your second
chakra as you release the energy lock.

After a few second chakra breaths, on the next inbreath,
again focus your attention on your root chakra, and as you
breathe in, pull your attention up, as if your attention were
the head of the kundalini serpent, and feel yourself rise to
your third chakra. Apply the root lock at the base of your

spine, hold your breath for a moment, and imagine seeing from your third chakra and its yellow lens. On the out-breath, imagine yourself breathing out a wave of energy from your third chakra.

For your fourth chakra, you apply the same technique and pull your attention, the head of your rising kundalini, to your heart chakra. Apply the root lock to hold the energy and then rest a moment in your heart. Some people see the color green through their heart chakra, while others see pink. What color comes to you today? Exhale and breathe out through your heart while radiating love. With an attitude of gratitude, breathe in the joy and love of who and what you are thankful for, and then on the outbreath, send this love out into the world.

Breathe in and apply the same technique for your fifth chakra at your throat. Apply the root lock and picture the color sky blue, and see what comes to you by raising your kundalini to your fifth chakra. The fifth chakra is sound vibration, and you can add the seed tone for vishuddha, *Ham* (pronounced "hum"), on your outbreath through your throat to further enhance this chakra.

For your sixth chakra, breathe in and pull your attention up to your third eye at the center of your forehead. Actually turn your eyes upward and toward the center of your forehead. Silently chant *Om* and focus on your third eye, visualizing the color indigo blue, and sense your separation from your body as you withdraw from sensory input. If you feel "floaty," enjoy the lift. You may choose to do several rounds with this chakra as you begin to actually experience the separation from outward senses and experience consciousness unfettered by worldly phenomena.

For your crown chakra, breathe in and pull your attention from the base of your spine all the way up to the white light of your crown, your connection to the spiritual source of all energy. Feel yourself open to this cosmic influx of energy. On the outbreath, feel this divine energy wash over you from your crown to the base of your spine, softening, melting tension, and purifying your karma at each chakra as its liquid light moves through your entire being. You may choose to do several rounds of this karma-cleansing, light-infusing crown chakra breathing and then sit with the spacious feeling that ensues. Relax your focus on the breath and just be.

To complete the meditation, take a few deep breaths and let your attention center on your heart chakra. Be thankful for your experience and feel the joy of knowing this connection and the peace it brings, which is always there. Rest in your heart, contemplating all that you are thankful for and appreciate in your life. Now take a few more deep breaths and prepare to begin the day with your awakened energy field.

Yogananda teaches that the practice of Kriya Yoga burns away your karma. Kriya Yoga activates the kundalini energy in the core of the sushumna channel, the core of your spine. Breathing, chanting *Om*, and invoking the divine blessing connects you with this channel that takes you to the place within you that is beyond personal karma—pure spirit. Breathing this awakened, pure spiritual energy up and down your spine helps purify your karma connected to each of your chakras.

Exercise
. . . .
The Microcosmic Orbit

The practice of the Microcosmic Orbit[10] uses breath and imagery to move the invisible life force of prana through a circuit in your body. To practice the Microcosmic Orbit, first visualize two energy channels for prana to move up and down your spine. The back channel starts at the perineum (between the anus and the genitals) and goes up the back of your spine, over the top of your head, down through your brow, and ends at the roof of your mouth. The front channel runs from your tongue, down through the throat and neck, through the heart, the stomach, and the genitals, and ends at the perineum. You complete the circuit by placing your tongue on the roof of your mouth.

First, sit in a comfortable meditation posture with your spine straight. Place your tongue on the roof of your mouth to connect the circuit and start the practice. On the inbreath, pull prana energy up through the back channel, from the base of the spine, up through the spine, over the top of your head, through your brow, and down to the roof of your mouth. On the outbreath, picture the prana moving down your tongue and throat, through your heart

---

10. This exercise is adapted from my book *Western Seeker, Eastern Paths* (St. Paul, MN: Llewellyn Publications, 2003).

and stomach, and past the genitals to the base of your spine. That is one round. Do several rounds.

Use imagery and trace the movement of the prana with your mind's eye. You can use a ball of light, a wave of energy, a comet, or whatever works for you. On the inbreath, pull the energy up the back of your spine, and on the outbreath, move it down the front. Feel the moving prana as cleansing and energizing your entire energy field. After several cycles, reverse the process and breath up through the front channel and down through the back channel. Again, picture the moving prana as both cleansing and revitalizing your entire energy field. Feel the yin-yang dance of your energy field—the female-male, the receptive-assertive—and feel these polarities blending and shifting into one another on the changing of the breath.

You can do this practice as long as you like. If you get dizzy or lightheaded, stop the practice and work on grounding yourself before you begin again. The practice serves as a general tonic to your energy field. Without discipline, the imagination leaks vital prana in its wandering; with a practice like the Microcosmic Orbit, your ability to visualize is trained to serve you in a revitalizing way.

The Microscopic Orbit exercise is particularly effective when you are feeling overwhelmed by the chaos of life. By creating a circuit for the prana to move through your entire energetic anatomy, you liberate energy from personal issues that are causing the feeling of being overwhelmed. When transformed through this practice, the same energy, which was previously overwhelming and chaotic, becomes the creative fuel of the higher mind.

Exercise
. . . .
The Inner Smile

This beautiful and simple practice can be integrated easily into your meditation practice. First close your eyes and imagine a friend, loved one, or favorite pet approaching you in your mind's eye, and feel a smile come over you. Visualize the energy of the smile coming through your eyes as if you were smiling through your eyes.

You can then take this energy of the smile on a journey through your chakras. Just as you pulled the energy of the smile into your eyes, focus the energy beam of the smile on the inside of your head and brain and smile through your sixth and seventh chakras. Smile through your fifth chakra at your throat. Smile from your chest and lungs and let the energy of your smile settle into your heart chakra. Enjoy a few breaths from your smiling heart, and then take the smile into your solar plexus and your third chakra. Smile into your second chakra in your lower abdomen and then into your first chakra at the base of the spine. Complete the meditation by feeling your entire body radiating the smile, and bask in this healing radiance.

Exercise
. . . .
Tune Your Spiritual Antenna Daily

Picture your spiritual eye as having an antenna that extends out into the collective astral plane. Imagine that you have been given a gift of an extremely sensitive radio that can pick up broadcasts from all over the world, from the most beautiful music and inspirational talks to all of the AM talk shows, news, and everything in between. The tuning dial of this receiver is so sensitive that it has to be adjusted daily to get the clearest reception. Now imagine that I visit you in your studio one day and, while walking in, I hear this awful static and screeching coming from the radio. The first thing you tell me is about how unsettling your day has been and that you just can't get focused. What would be my advice? The most obvious advice would be to point out the source of the obnoxious sounds: the receiver needs adjusting to tune it to something more enchanting.

And so it is with the spiritual antenna of your spiritual eye. You could have walked with the masters in meditation yesterday, but without tuning your spiritual antenna today, you will be just as lost as ever. You don't have to get to a deep meditative place each day to stay tuned. A simple morning affirmation of your intention to tune in to your Higher Self made in earnest, such as the following one, will work:

May I be aligned with my Higher Self today and that which is in my soul's best interest and in the best interests of the people I love as well.

. . . .

Additional Activities to Enhance Your Sixth Chakra

Chant *Om* silently to generate supporting fifth chakra energy. Then just sit and focus on your third eye and be with the divine grace.

Affirmations for Your Sixth Chakra

Whether this day brings ups or downs, joys or sorrows, I am able to withdraw my mind from worldly concerns and focus on the light of my inner vision.

May I be purified of the imperfections that cloud the vision of the lotus flower of my spiritual eye.

May I align with the original purity of being as I reach for the light.

Mantras

Om; Om Mani Padme Hum ("May I align with perfect existence in the jewel of the lotus flower I am").

Self-Massage

Massage and tap with your fingers your medulla (the hollow at the base of your skull) with palms over ears (beating the heavenly drum).

Massage and tap the front of the brow at your third eye, and then your temples near the sides of your eyes.

With eyes open, roll your eyes upward and look to the center of your brow. Practice getting comfortable with this upward gazing, then close your eyes, still looking up at your third eye inwardly.

Yoga Postures

Lotus pose, head-to-knee pose, downward facing dog, and child's pose all facilitate bringing your attention to your sixth chakra. During your postures, you could silently chant *Om*, the seed sound for the sixth chakra, while focusing on the light of your spiritual eye at your brow.

Body Associations

The eyes, nose, sinuses, automatic nervous system, cerebellum, forebrain, and pineal gland are all associated with the sixth chakra. Difficulties with any of these are indications of an imbalance in your sixth chakra.

Sixth Chakra Foods

The element of light of your sixth chakra is fed by light meals and indigo and purple vegetables. Eggplant, purple kale, purple cabbage, wheat germ, Concord grapes, blueberries, lavender, alfalfa, chamomile, and vitamin E all enhance your sixth chakra. Sixth chakra treats include red wine and chocolate, while incense and candles can also feed your sixth chakra.

Sixth Chakra Journaling

After reading about your sixth chakra, this would be a good time to stop and contemplate your experiences with your inner vision. Have you taken time to become familiar with your Observer within to know the peace and tranquility that come from its awakening? Have you been allowing your imagination to run wild, or have you been directing it toward inspirational sources? In your journal, record the insights you get from your Higher Self as to how you can improve your inner vision.

CHAPTER 8

Seventh Chakra: Sahasrara

Location: Crown

Element: Empty space

Symbol: A thousand-petaled lotus blossom

Key Benefits: Merging with the spiritual source and living a spiritually infused life

Key Difficulty: Disassociation from reality

Spiritual Quality: Seeing spiritual essence animating all of creation

Colors: Clear light, white, and violet

Function: Pure consciousness

Types of Intelligence: Silence and the source of all intelligence

Your crown chakra is where your Higher Self merges with the spiritual source of all life. You realize, from this unitive state of consciousness, that this same sacred life force flows through all of creation. The meaning of *sahasrara*, and the symbol for your crown chakra, is the thousand-petaled lotus flower, the final blossoming of spiritual consciousness. It relates to pure consciousness, and it is from this chakra that all the other chakras emanate.

Rising out of the sixth chakra, all illusions of separateness disappear into the realization that you have never been separate from the divine source any more than a wave can be separate from the ocean. The oceanic level of consciousness of your crown chakra realizes that it is all the same ocean.

A key attribute of your crown chakra is transcendence, the pathway to your spiritual source. Your crown chakra transcends all dualities—not just integrating duality, as with your heart chakra, but transcending duality. Even the Observer, which is necessary to rise out of an ego-dominated perspective, drops away as the final veil and you become absorbed into the universal source energy, the non-dual state where subject and object become as one. The call of your seventh chakra is to experience the freedom, profundity, and bliss of your spiritual nature.

All limitations of space and time are transcended from your crown chakra, giving you access to the same enlightened wisdom that masters of all ages have drawn from. This wisdom is available not only to saints and sages but to all people. From your crown chakra, you become aware of the formless, the limitless void, and its doorway to the infinite—the unchanging, timeless nature of your spiritual self that is not embodied, never born, never dying.

This highest spiritual awakening is called many names the world over. Enlightenment, Christ consciousness, Buddhahood, God-realization, universal consciousness, samadhi, Atman, the Tao, oneness, unity, rigpa, and Big Sky Mind are some of the names we give to awakening to the peak state of the crown chakra.

Enlightened Moments

Although enlightenment may seem out of reach for most of us mere mortals, *enlightened moments* you can expect from an open crown chakra. Enlightened moments are the rare special moments that occur out of the blue when you get absorbed in the enlightened state, seeing deep into the meaning of life with startling clarity. These special moments don't last, but working with your crown chakra helps create the space in your psyche for these enlightened moments to occur more frequently.

Where volumes can be written about the kaleidoscopic sixth chakra, with all of its many and wondrous possibilities, less can be written about the seventh. How do you describe pure light before the prism of the chakras fragments the wholeness into its distinguishable colors and frequencies? As is said of the mysterious Tao, "Those who know don't say; those who say don't know," and this points to the difficulties of describing the crown chakra. Beyond its attributes, this chakra is indescribable by its very nature; if you know it, that is not it—it being the source of knowing. Knowing is one of the seventh chakra's expressions, but the source can't be known by what it creates. Source energy is transcendent of both grammar and thoughts; thus, describing it is like a poet trying to put the smell of a rose in a poem.

To awaken to your crown chakra is to become comfortable with the unknowable. If you know it, that is not it; if it knows you, you've got it. You can't know the unlimited from the limited. Stay in the mystery to feel its presence. Your connection to the divine source of all life can never be attained, achieved, earned, or lost; it is always there. You can't think your way to your crown chakra; you sense your way to its mysterious presence.

The purpose of yoga, union with the divine, can be experienced at sahasrara. The highest state of meditation, *nirvikalpa samadhi*,[11] is of the crown chakra, where the knower, the act of knowing, and the object known all become absorbed into one undifferentiated state of pure consciousness.

As you awaken into oneness at your seventh chakra, individual karma drops away. In oneness, everything is the cause of everything. Everything in all times and places is part of the one. Each moment is caused by and interrelated with every other moment, and the idea of personal karma, as if one action caused such and such, disappears. *Samskaras*, the latent impressions of unacted-upon desires, are burned up; the *vrittis*[12] of mental activity are calmed; and *moksha*,[13] the final release, is experienced.

The teachings on moksha suggest that upon experiencing this final merging with the divine, you then become liberated from the wheel of death and rebirth, as if you were to leave this earthly abode, never to return.

For those of us who plan on sticking around, applying the principle of moksha in your meditation practice is to know that experiencing this highest state of union with the divine liberates you *at least for this day* from the karma that previously needed to be worked through. Moksha gives you the freedom to reenter the world with true free will, not being tugged and pulled by unconscious desires and drives.

---

11. Alistair Shearer, trans. and intro., *The Yoga Sutras of Patanjali* (New York: Bell Tower, 1982).

12. *Vrittis* are the waves or whirlpools of consciousness that disturb its calm nature. In the *Yoga Sutras,* Patanjali defines *yoga* as the process of calming these waves to reunite with one's spiritual essence.

13. *Moksha* is the final liberation from the wheel of birth and death.

Incorporating glimpses that you get into your infinite spiritual essence while living in a finite body is the work of the seventh chakra. The following sections on silence, the mysterious void, and surrendering to your soul's purpose will further explore your connection to your spiritual source.

Silence

Silence is the virtue of your crown chakra and is the surest way to come to know this chakra—silencing not just the outer tongue but also the inner voices of unceasing self-dialogue. Your attention must be withdrawn from this incessant chatter to hear the silent whispers from the divine.

Cultivating your relationship with silence as an inner refuge from the world gives you a home base to return to that is not dependent on outer circumstances. Resting in pure awareness born of silence becomes an inner resource. From this inner refuge of silence, you are aware of the constant movement of thoughts without getting trapped by them. You are aware of the rising and falling of emotions without becoming engulfed in their currents. You see the entire ever-changing phenomenal world from the vantage point of simple aware presence, the awakened state. This resting in simple awareness of presence becomes an inner resource that is always accessible.

The Mysterious Void
and Its Eternal Potential

The divine source of all of creation is forever unknown, invisible, and yet is full to the brim with pure potential and is constantly coming into existence. The mysterious void is an ocean of pure existence, pure intelligence, an alive, bubbling sea of the unmanifest existing as pure potentiality.

In the materialistic era that we have been immersed in, acquiring things is what our culture has been focused on. Even science had been harnessed in the pre-quantum era to look exclusively at physical matter to understand truth. This has led to a residual prevailing cultural attitude about the principle of emptiness that has derogatory associations: absence of value, nothing there, the opposite of full—and full is good, so empty is bad. An empty gas tank, empty stomach, or empty wallet is certainly nothing one would aspire to.

We need more words to describe the various types of emptiness. It is not a "one word fits all" situation when so many of the Eastern teachings about consciousness development hold emptiness in the highest esteem as the source of all of creation.

This is the emptiness of Rumi's flute, which allows life to flow through you unimpaired, and is certainly not the empty-wallet type of emptiness. The emptiness of sahasrara is the pregnant void that all is born from and returns to. It is the wellspring of all creativity and inspired activity. It is the still, quiet moment within that reveals the sudden inspiration and revelation about something you have been puzzling over.

When you are empty and not full of yourself, life can happen. Otherwise, it is just you acting out your futile plan to harness and control reality. You need to travel to the heights of your seventh chakra to find this place in consciousness that is empty, but is full to the brim with potentiality.

the Fool, 22

Nirvana

Nirvana is often associated with the bliss of experiencing the transcendent state of divine union. The meaning of the word *nirvana* is "to blow out the flame of desire." The bliss associated with nirvana comes from being desireless, and, as the definition reveals, the flame of desire is blown out rather than magically disappearing. To blow out is an act of volition; and to stay in the peace of sahasrara, purposefully snuff out distracting desires when they do emerge.

As you deepen your connection to your crown chakra, the desireless state of bliss occurs spontaneously and disrupting desires essentially melt away. When they do arise, they are easy to blow out, not by repressing them but by simply dismissing them.

Nisargadatta, a great teacher from India, describes an awakened crown chakra with this beautiful quote: "When I look inside myself, I see that I am nothing, and that is wisdom; when I look outside, I see that I am everything, and that is love. And between these two shores, my life exists." [14]

Your Personal Battle with Mara

In the story of Buddha's awakening, as the Buddha was sitting off by himself on the verge of his ultimate awakening, Mara, the tempter, kept interrupting his meditation with various seductive promises and allurements. The Buddha held his ground, won the battle, and awakened.

For most of us, awakening is not permanent, as it was with the Buddha. You must win this battle every day when some visitation

---

14. Sri Nisargadatta Maharaj, *I Am That* (1973; reprint, Durham, NC: Acorn Press, 1982).

from your own personal Mara tempts you with enticing promises of the lower chakras. In that moment, choose the love of the divine. That's the battle and the moment of choice each day.

Surrendering to Your Soul's Purpose

A familiar hunger to many seekers on the path of consciousness growth is to know their soul's purpose. Unconditional surrender is required to live a life directed by your soul's calling—surrender not as giving up but surrendering your will and consciousness to a higher power. To know your soul's purpose, you must surrender unconditionally to its guidance. Conditional surrendering would be something along these lines: "I would like to surrender to my soul's purpose as long as I can have a good income, relationship, etc." This is still directing the soul rather than being directed by it.

To fully surrender is to know that your soul's purpose would always include the best interests of the people you love as well. You don't have to make that a condition; it is a condition of your soul's purpose.

I felt the call of my soul's purpose early in life. As a young family man, I had envisioned myself becoming a schoolteacher and coach to provide for my family. After a few years in the classroom, although I felt proud and honorable about the career path I had chosen, I still felt overly confined by the school system and found myself being more interested in my students' astrology charts than in their math scores! Leaving the security of the salaried life of a teacher to pursue the uncertain career of an astrologer when I had a family to provide for was a test of faith for sure.

When I asked to surrender to my soul's purpose, it was easy for me to see my consuming passion was in matters of consciousness, and a career as an astrologer would allow for that. Also, I was getting feedback from the people whose astrology charts I interpreted that I had some talent in giving readings, and I was delighted to explore all the realms of consciousness with my clients that an astrology reading entails. It was easy for me to see that this path fit for me, but I had a growing family to provide for, and an astrology career seemed to offer no assurance of a reliable income.

It was a leap of faith to surrender to the calling of my soul's purpose, but now, forty years later, I can say that the path of following my soul's calling has created a life for us that is far greater than I could have imagined myself attaining. It's not that money has just appeared at the right time, but the opportunity to earn it has. Laurie and I together have had to learn to manage the business side of an astrology practice, and both of us put in an honest workweek to maintain it. Even though we have never had work scheduled for much more than a few weeks out, and often not much scheduled even the following week, the work always shows up and the schedule fills. Following this path has allowed us to have a very decent lifestyle, even abundant in our eyes, and I am forever grateful to have a life partner who has been strong enough of faith to take this step with me.

There was a time early in my career as an astrologer and writer when I felt compelled to go back to college to pursue a master of science degree in experimental metaphysics. The compelling nature of the call assured me that it was coming from my Higher Self and my desire to surrender to my soul's purpose. I had already been practicing astrology for many years and was experiencing success, but I wanted to know more about how and why astrology worked scientifically.

This call came at a very busy time in my life. I was married, had four young sons, and owned and operated a restaurant to provide for my family, practicing astrology on the side. To think about taking on a two-year master's degree program on top of an already quite busy life seemed rather ludicrous, but consistently, after meditating, the call persisted.

I said to my Higher Self, "Okay, well then you are going to have to help me," and so it did. Before important tests when I would have precious little time to study, I would first meditate and then ask my Higher Self to help me prepare for the test. I would begin to study and essentially let the book fall open and then pour into the material that caught my eye. Just before the exam, I would again meditate and picture the professor shaking my hand and saying "well done," and then I would go take the exam. Invariably, the material I was led to study the night before made up the core of the exam and I was able to pass successfully.

Seventh Chakra Difficulties and Solutions

If you are blocked at your crown chakra, you can feel disconnected to spirit and likely have a cynical view of all things spiritual, which can result in loneliness, depression, or a strong fear of death. When the crown chakra is open but not integrated with the rest of the chakras, disassociation of one type or another is likely, making it difficult to function in society.

Diminished Seventh Chakra

If there is under-activity or a blockage in your crown chakra, you will likely feel like you lack purpose in life. You may think that life is meaningless, or you may feel unloved or angry at God or blame the circumstances of your life on something that is outside of you. With a blocked crown chakra, you lack spiritual exploration and likely have no interest in discovering your inner self. Cut off from your eternal spiritual nature, you can have a fear of aging and a morbid view of death.

As you awaken to your crown chakra and your connection to the eternal source beyond your body, death is seen as another doorway, but until awakening, you are likely to be cynical about all things spiritual. You first look for truth with your mind, and if your mind can't understand the information, you discount it as irrelevant at best or with scornful rejection at worst.

A tragedy can trigger a separation from God. While with an open crown chakra, a person's faith in the divine can be their saving grace that pulls them through a tragic loss, those with a closed crown chakra become even angrier with God or use the tragedy as evidence that there is no God.

This is the ego trying to understand why God would allow such a tragedy to happen. The mind will never be able to understand the mysteries of the crown chakra; it is of a different order, beyond the range of the mind. As with sight, our eyes pick up only a small range of the total electromagnetic energy field—and so it is with the mind. Its range limits its capacity to know the workings of the spiritual world. The mind's function is to serve your body and its needs.

Divinely Inspired Wounds

With some wounds in life, through the healing of the wound, we are set on a path that is better suited to our Higher Self. We could call these divinely inspired wounds. Imagine that a person goes through a painful divorce and, after floundering in the wound, is eventually drawn to the process of healing and facing the issues within that were problematic in the relationship. After experiencing the personal growth and development it takes to heal the wound, the person attracts a relationship that has qualities they were not even aware of before. This is a divinely inspired wound, and it is helpful to acknowledge this by going back and removing the thorn from your memory. We are thankful for some wounding experiences later, after life changes for the better. These experiences help get us back in the good graces of the mysterious workings of the spiritual in our lives.

Excessive Crown Chakra Issues

An over-active focus on your crown chakra can lead to an obsessive attachment to spiritual matters, making you feel that you are just too sensitive for the harsh realities of life. You can be considered by others to be out of touch with reality—if your spiritual awareness is not balanced with a healthy personal life, it can be hard for others to take you seriously. Awakening to your seventh chakra without integrating it with your other chakras can lead to a God complex and feelings of being superior to the rest of the world.

Former Harvard professor, author, and revered teacher Ram Dass tells the story of visiting his brother who was sent to live in an asylum because of such a God complex.[15] This was shortly after Ram Dass had taken on his new spiritual name given to him by his guru. The hippie movement and the consciousness movement came together for a time in the sixties, and Ram Dass had hair past his shoulders and a long beard, wore beads, and was dressed in a skirt. His brother looked at him and asked the question, "Why am I in here and you are free? You are the one that is dressed like a nutcase." Ram Dass asked his brother if he believed he was God, to which his brother responded, "Yes." Ram Dass then asked if he believed anyone else was God, to which his brother responded, "No." Ram Dass then said, "You believe you are God, but that nobody else is. I also believe I am God, but I believe everyone else is too. That difference is why you are in here and I am out in the world free."

Activities to Empower Your Seventh Chakra

Having a regular meditation practice is a sure path for energizing your seventh chakra. From the preceding sixth chakra, you guide your meditation with breath, attention, and visualization, setting the stage for the final stage of meditation at the crown chakra: absorption. For absorption into spirit to take place, you drop all the techniques you use to direct the meditation and enter into pure listening. In the guided prayers and meditations from the sixth chakra, you are asking something of God and your Higher Self, and at the seventh chakra you listen for the answer.

Joining other spiritually minded individuals at spiritual gatherings, from a church service to meditation class, supports many

---

15. Ram Dass, from the transcription of a lecture given to the Menninger Foundation in Topeka, Kansas, on May 5, 1970.

people in maintaining their connection to spirit, while other people prefer quiet time alone to hear these whispers.

When you are experiencing life from your crown chakra and resting in pure awareness, you experience a natural ease and sense of well-being. From here you accept life on its terms, rather than trying to mold it to your desires. Learn to trust this state of pure awareness as your norm. Then whenever you experience the stress, worry, anxiety, or doubt arising from your lower chakras, notice the constrictive energy immediately as an inner alarm letting you know you are wandering from your inner truth. Hear the alarm, make the adjustment by disbelieving your ego's current story of dissatisfaction, *drop it,* and return to the well-being of your spirit within.

One way that I use my crown chakra is in initiating an astrology reading for a distant client. After preparing my client's astrology chart and familiarizing myself with the core themes, I then initiate the reading with a little ritual. I center myself with a few deep breaths, then look at the picture of my spiritual teacher and invite him into my heart. Next I picture an aquamarine light coming to me from above, activating my throat chakra so that I might be a voice for what my client needs to hear. I next picture an indigo ray of light activating my spiritual eye, then I sit in silence for just a moment and say my opening invocation silently to myself:

May my Higher Self connect with the Higher Self of my client and lead me to the information that will be most helpful, loving, and uplifting.

It is my spiritual eye that directs the intention, and it is the empty space of my crown chakra that the prayer moves through. The same empty space that flows through you and me flows through all of creation and is the matrix that weaves it all together.

Exercise
· ·
Alternate Nostril Breathing

Practice alternate nostril breathing to bring the receptive and active energy channels of your energy field into balance at your sixth chakra, then picture them rising together to receive the light of your crown chakra.

Sit with your spine straight, as if you were preparing to meditate. Place your right thumb on your right nostril and your right ring finger on your left nostril, with your right middle and index fingers together and resting on your brow.

Take a few deep, centering breaths, then on your next inbreath, close your right nostril with your thumb, and as you breathe in through your open left nostril, picture filling your feminine, receptive energy channel (ida) with prana. Picture filling yourself with receptive yin energy on your left side; start from your first chakra and pull the energy upward to the center of your brow with your inbreath. Now close your left nostril with your ring finger while opening your right nostril, and as you breathe out, picture yourself emptying your masculine action channel (pingala) of all tensions and pressures from your brow to your first chakra on your right side.

Now on the next inbreath, keep your left nostril closed and your right nostril open while picturing yourself filling your right channel with prana, strength, and courage. Pull your attention and this assertive energy to your third eye, and see it merging with the receptive, feminine energy. Close your right nostril and now breathe out of your left nostril, emptying your feminine ida channel of all emotional concerns and relationship issues.

Repeat this cycle seven times, then drop your right hand onto your lap and direct your attention to your crown, relax your breath, and sit with this balanced, spacious energy. Feel an open and expanded sensation at the top of your head. Feel your oneness and unity with all of life. Feel your connection to a force of life greater than yourself. Affirm: "I am connected to a life force greater than myself and know that I am never alone."

. . . .

Community of Higher Selves

When we lived in Hawaii, I had the opportunity to make the acquaintance of a few of the local kahunas, the priests and shamans of the ancient Hawaiian teachings. I was drawn to study their system of knowledge about the workings of the unseen world. Their teaching on the *community of Higher Selves* [16] is a marvelous way of utilizing your crown chakra.

Kahuna belief echoes many cultures' beliefs that we all have a Lower Self, a Personal Self, and a Higher Self. When you make a goal or say a prayer from your Personal Self that is in alignment with your Higher Self, it is then your Higher Self's responsibility to assist you in achieving your ambition. When your goal includes the best interests of others, those people's Higher Selves join in community with your Higher Self to support your efforts. The more people there are who would benefit from you achiev-

---

16. Max Freedom Long, *The Secret Science Behind Miracles* (Marina Del Rey, CA: DeVorss, 1953).

ing your goal, the wider will be the circle of the community of Higher Selves assisting you.

Imagine you are surrendering to your soul's calling to be a midwife and are pursuing your training. Contemplate all of the people who will be helped by you being successful at your goal. Trust that their Higher Selves will be part of your community of Higher Selves to assist you along the way.

Additional Activities to Enhance Your Seventh Chakra

Yoga Postures

Inversions, headstand, and lotus posture for meditation are all beneficial for the seventh chakra. While doing your postures, slow down your practice and focus on your connection to the universal life source infusing your being with its spiritual light.

Affirmations for Your Seventh Chakra

I AM pure consciousness manifesting my mind, my body, my thoughts and emotions. I AM something much larger and more mysterious than these expressions of who I AM.

Breathing in, I am stillness,
Breathing out, I am One.

Body Associations

The upper brain, cerebral cortex, cerebrum, central nervous system, and top of the head are associated with the seventh chakra. Headaches and other difficulties with these parts of the body indicate difficulties with your crown chakra.

Seventh Chakra Foods

Your crown chakra is fed more by spiritual activity, such as prayer and meditation, than by physical food. Light meals, fasting, and juicing can benefit your crown chakra's opening to its nourishment—the descent of spiritual essence into your being. "Silence outside, silence inside" is a sure tonic for your seventh chakra. This creates the openness for the light of spirit to fully enter you, feeding your entire being with your true spiritual essence.

Seventh Chakra Gemstones and Crystals

Amethyst, clear quartz, and diamond resonate with your crown chakra. Use purple amethyst for spiritual purification and clear quartz or diamond to animate your seventh chakra.

Seventh Chakra Journaling

Stop now and contemplate your connection to your seventh chakra and your openness to its spiritual essence. After reading about your crown chakra, what insights have you gained that would be helpful to record in your journal? Did you get nudges from your Higher Self as to what would be helpful for you to integrate into your life? Pay special attention to your unique insights that are born from the material in this book but are not in this book. Don't let these become insights you wish you had remembered later, but they just got away. Record these nuggets and you will have them available as resources later when you want to remember one of these flashes.

Now that you have worked through your entire chakra system, stop and reflect on your energetic anatomy as a whole.

Which are your favorite chakras and which are your least favorite? Which ones did you have difficulty connecting with, and which ones could you readily incorporate into your understanding of life? Have you been like a chakra amputee, finding fulfillment in some of your chakras but feeling entirely cut off from others? The full light of your being shines through when all of your chakras are open and supporting each other. You may have a natural preference and inclination for specific chakras, but remembering to keep your whole system open brings even more energy to your favorite chakras. As you picture your energetic system as a whole, ask yourself where you could benefit by directing attention to neglected chakras in your life, then record your insights.

CONCLUSION
....
After Awakening
to the Power Within

After awakening to the power within all of your chakras, you will no longer be dependent on outer circumstances for your happiness, fulfillment, and sense of well-being, having discovered these within yourself. Your relationship with life and others will take on a new quality of freshness and discovery. Spontaneous joy and spontaneous love will become frequent visitors in your life, as you have learned to seek out the spiritual light hidden within all of creation. Life will open up before you in ways your ego never could have imagined. It is the same world after awakening, but now you experience it in a whole new way. T. S. Eliot expressed this eloquently: "We shall not cease from exploration, and the end of all our exploring will be to arrive where we started and know the place for the first time."[17]

However, even after awakening to the highest states of your crown chakra, the work is not complete once and for all. You will

---

17. T. S. Eliot, *Four Quartets*, Section V (New York: Harcourt Brace, 1943).

be open, with life flowing through you more often, but you will still have periods of feeling blocked and closed when your lower chakras interrupt your peace. After awakening to the clarity of experiencing your open energy field and your familiarity with each of your chakras, you will know immediately the moment your energy field closes and specifically which of your chakras is demanding attention.

After the honeymoon of awakening begins the marriage of integrating your awakened awareness into all aspects of your life. The honeymoon holds all of the promise, and the marriage is the work of constantly polishing and refining your skill at moving freely throughout the energetic spectrum of your being.

After awakening to your essential truth through direct experience, you no longer aspire toward a mental image or concept of awakening. Now you know truth experientially, and you can only embody what you know through experience. Now you are able to express in the world the peace, love, awareness, and spiritual wisdom that you are discovering within yourself. You can now live the deepest truth you know.

There is a famous Zen parable about a scholar of religious studies at a local university who became upset over hearing about the great respect some of his students had for a local Zen monk. To investigate further, he arranged a meeting with the monk. As they sat down for tea, the monk poured. When serving the scholar, the monk kept pouring even after the cup was full, and it began spilling over. Shocked, the scholar exclaimed, "My cup is already full!" As the monk set down the teapot, he replied, "Just as you are, my friend. You are full of self-knowledge and not able to receive more."

After awakening, you are no longer full of yourself and you can receive from life's bounty. "The great way is not difficult for those who have no preferences," [18] a Zen patriarch once proclaimed.

The work of integrating your awakening into your everyday life is to stay aware and unconflicted within yourself throughout the nitty-gritty moments that make up your day of interacting with a largely unawakened world. Revelatory moments are rare— life is made up mostly of small moments. Embodying your truth is one thing during a walk through the park but quite another in the marketplace, in traffic, or at the workplace. This is where the proverbial rubber hits the road of embodying your awakening.

Living a Spiritually Infused Life

On the ascent through your chakras toward aligning with your spiritual essence, you see your spiritual life as one of the compartments of your life: "This is my work life, this is my personal life, this is my relationship life, and this is my spiritual life." After awakening, you no longer look to the spiritual only when you are in need or in crisis; you now see the luminous presence of the divine spirit throughout all of creation. As your connection to spirit deepens, it infuses all aspects of your life and becomes seamlessly woven into all that you do.

Our modern human tribe in general lacks a core connection to the spiritual source within, which is what brings peace to troubled hearts and awakens spiritual values. There is plenty being taught

---

18. Seng-ts'an, *Hsin-Hsin Ming: Verses on the Faith-Mind*, trans. Richard B. Clarke (Buffalo, NY: White Pine Press, 2001).

about how one should live a moral life and what one should or shouldn't do, but it is an imposed, outside-in morality.

Imposed morality transforms into inherent morality after awakening. The universal qualities of compassion, love, peace, clarity, and wisdom naturally flow from an awakened individual as core qualities. A person who has awakened to their spiritual core is loving, kind, and wise without effort. Having tamed your inner chaos, you have an openness and a space within your psyche to help others.

Bringing your spiritual awakening into each of your chakras allows you to experience them in a whole new light. Obscurations are removed, allowing them to operate in their natural, healthy manner, with the full radiance of your spirit shining through all you do.

First Chakra

Bringing your awakened spiritual awareness into your first chakra transforms your experience of being in a body. You enjoy and feel great gratitude for your body as your spirit's vehicle for experiencing this physical incarnation. You have learned that infusing infinite spirit into your finite body includes honoring your body's limits, and you listen to its instincts for guidance to keep it healthy. Having met the security needs of your first chakra through your connection to your spiritual essence, you are no longer dependent on material circumstances for your sense of feeling safe and secure. Not being attached to money and possessions has created a new openness to receiving the flow of prosperity in your life.

Second Chakra

With awakening, you have found the place within you that knows how to enjoy without being dependent on what it enjoys. You have learned to experience the full range of your emotions without getting lost in them. Without the attachments or aversions of the pleasure-seeking second chakra, you delightfully surrender to your sensuality and sexuality when situations present themselves, and you have quieted the desire for them when they are not there. You have grown to expect change as the natural order of things and are able to fluidly adapt to ever-changing reality.

Third Chakra

Bringing your awakened awareness to your power chakra activates your spiritual will and gives you the ability to exercise self-control and to focus your will into action. You have learned how to assert your will when appropriate and how to relax it when it is not necessary. Your self-esteem comes from aligning with the calling of your Higher Self, no longer dependent on achieving recognition nor fearing failure. You have learned the secret of manifesting your goals by approaching them with the satisfaction you would feel as if you had already achieved them. Bringing the feeling of fulfillment into the here and now helps you manifest your goals.

Fourth Chakra

After awakening, you have found the place within you that knows how to love independent of the actions of others. No longer reaching for love, you are now full of love and gladly share with others from this fullness. You have mastered the art of being skillfully compassionate and are able to touch other people's troubled hearts with mercy in a way that is healing and uplifting. Having learned the skill of rising above your personal preferences, you stay in open acceptance of others and of life itself, which allows you to live with joy and abundance.

Fifth Chakra

With your awakened fifth chakra, you have found your intuitive direct sense of truth that is not dependent on anyone else's beliefs. You have liberated yourself from excessive concerns over how others think of you and are free to express yourself. More interested in insights than mental banter, you have learned to listen attentively to others and let the fullness of their message impact you before responding with your personal reaction. You have grown to trust that truth stands on its own merit, needing no justification nor argument to verify it. Your insights born in the moment often cut through the belief systems of others, giving them startling new insights into their own lives.

Sixth Chakra

You have found the Observer within residing in your awakened sixth chakra. Here you see things as they are without judgment. From here you are able to experience peace and tranquility without needing the world to be peaceful and tranquil. You have learned to master your ability to imagine and visualize, and are no longer plagued by imagined fears, escapism, or excessive fantasizing. You have trained your spiritual eye to direct your imagination away from these distractions and look instead toward your spiritual source—filling you with light, inspiration, and intuitive knowledge. You are simply being, but to those still directed by distraction, you seem like a modern-day Jedi knight, able to sense and direct "the Force."

Seventh Chakra

Your awakened seventh chakra manifests as your constant awareness of the source of all your power within—the source of even the Observer. As your sense of "I am" merges with the source of creation, seeking dissolves into union. That which has been sought after has been found within, and life begins to coalesce around this awakened state.

Reentering the World after Awakening

After you reach the pinnacle of consciousness, life will invariably call you back from your detached peak to reenter the world. On the ascent of discovering the power within, *disengaging* from the world is the way, while on the descent back into your life, *engaging* with the world becomes the way. The ascent most often requires spiritual practices and disciplines to harness the wild mind in order to shift your self-identity from your Personal Self to your Higher Self. On the descent, you seek soul-nurturing activities more than disciplined practices to align with your spiritual essence.

Spiritual awakening is often therapeutic at first, healing the wounds of a life void of spirit. After applying the discipline that it takes for your self-identity to become anchored in your Higher Self, you may find that this disciplined practice to get to your spiritual abode is not as essential. Once you are in Chicago, you no longer need to take a bus to Chicago.

The need for disciplined spiritual practice gives way to the delight in taking part in soul-enriching, spirit-enhancing activities. Taking a walk in nature, reading sacred literature, or listening to music or inspired speakers all become avenues for getting to the same "absorbed in spirit" place that once required disciplined practices to attain.

After awakening to the power within, you bring your awareness into everything you do. Stay aware while being involved—that's all. This totally changes the quality of your participation with life and others.

Awakening is not simply passively accepting everything and everybody. This becomes an active openness that changes the quality of your involvement with all of life. Life isn't as hard when you no longer feel like you are pushing it up a hill. You use your will to participate in your life with a greater sense of ease.

After awakening, you no longer relate to others through your mental image of who you think they are; you naturally become more interested in what the other person is expressing in the here and now than in any agenda of your own. Not filling the space with your own agenda creates a new openness and aliveness in your relationships with all of life. Now the attitude of discovery animates your involvement with others.

After awakening, your life path appears like a maze in front of you. This maze is invisible, and the walls are like an invisible electric fence that will shock you if you bump into it. Not liking shocks, you get better and better at sensing the approaching electric fence. By becoming aware of the field around you, you learn to adjust your course before you get shocked. You sense the smooth channel by feeling when you are drifting away from it, like an elastic band that is getting stretched.

On an everyday level, you can bring your awakened and aware consciousness into all that you do throughout the day. Simply staying aware and mindful of your energy while you are involved in the activities of your life, even in a difficult moment with another person, will pull you back to your center quickly. It is that simple and accessible. Your awareness is always centered and non-reactive. Your ego isn't, but when you stay consciously aware of your energy while experiencing your ego's reactions, you don't remain stuck in polarities and your awareness pulls you back to your center.

After awakening, the level of discourse changes in your presence while interacting with others. Even without you directing the conversation, others simply aren't as inclined to engage in less-than-honorable topics of discussion.

Siddhis: Gifts of Spirit

Siddhis, from the yogic tradition, are the special abilities and seemingly magical powers that can naturally arise from clearing your upper chakras and awakening to your Higher Self. After awakening, your range of perception extends beyond your senses. Skills such as telepathy, intuition, astral travel, remote viewing, the ability to communicate with those who have crossed over, accessing other levels of intelligence, and the development of healing abilities are examples of particular siddhis that can naturally come to you after awakening.

These gifts of spirit are not just for the individual who is awakening to a special talent. Gifts of spirit are also for those who can benefit from your awakened talents. Others will recognize your gift and seek your assistance in their lives. You have learned the wisdom of not offering spiritual counsel to others without their asking, but when asked, you are more than happy to help as best you can.

Soul Purpose after Awakening

After awakening, your hunger to know your soul purpose drops— because you are living it. The question of "what should I do with my life?" transforms into "what is life asking of me and how can I contribute to this moment?" You have shifted from searching for something from life to having found great treasures within, and you are now looking for ways to share what you have found to help others.

Be a Demonstration of Your Awakening

After awakening, the paradigm shift that began in your heart chakra of greater acceptance of life has blossomed into all areas of life. While the world around you may be living with the fear, scarcity, and lack mentality of the unawakened state of consciousness, you live a life of faith, acceptance, and abundance. The desire to help alleviate the suffering that exists in the world most often arises after having found inner peace. There is always a way to help lift the spirits of the world.

When I was a young astrologer, in my twenties, I was giving a public talk on astrology at the restaurant we owned. Most of those in attendance were young hippies, with the exception of one lady who appeared to be in her eighties. She was dressed quite properly, making her stand out all the more in the group.

She sat by herself at a table and remained calm and still throughout the presentation.

After the talk, I approached her and asked if she would join me for a cup of tea. I was quite curious as to what had brought her to the talk. She told me that she had always enjoyed all things metaphysical and spiritual and was quite knowledgeable in astrology herself. She had long ago retired, and I asked her what she liked to do now.

She confided that having found such great peace in her life, she wanted to somehow help those who were struggling in their lives. She lived on a hilltop above the valley community, and in the evening when people were arriving home from work, she would play her piano and picture the music flowing out over the valley and calming the people of the town after their stressful day.

As you awaken to the fullness of who you are, may the music of your being help lift the spirits of our troubled world. There is always a way.

Suggested Reading

Adyashanti. *Falling into Grace.* Boulder, CO: Sounds True, 2011.

Bancroft, Anne, ed. *The Dhammapada.* Rockport, MA: Element, 1997.

Barks, Coleman, trans. *The Essential Rumi.* San Francisco, CA: Harper, 1995.

Brennan, Barbara Ann. *Hands of Light.* New York: Bantam Books, 1988.

Carter, Rita. *The Human Brain.* New York: DK Publishing, 2009.

Chodron, Pema. *When Things Fall Apart.* Boston, MA: Shambhala Publications, 1997.

Dalai Lama. *Awakening the Mind, Lightening the Heart.* New York: HarperSanFrancisco, 1995.

———. *The Power of Compassion.* New York: HarperCollins, 1995.

Easwaran, Eknath, trans. *The Bhagavad Gita.* Tomales, CA: Nilgiri Press, 1985.

Eden, Donna, with David Feinstein. *Energy Medicine*. New York: Jeremy P. Tarcher/Putnam, 1998.

Fox, Matthew. *Creativity*. New York: Jeremy P. Tarcher/Putnam, 2002.

Howe, Linda. *How to Read the Akashic Records*. Boulder, CO: Sounds True, 2009.

Judith, Anodea. *Wheels of Life*. St. Paul, MN: Llewellyn, 1997.

Jung, C. G. *Memories, Dreams, Reflections*. New York: Vintage Books, 1961.

Krishnamurti, J. *Think On These Things*. New York: HarperCollins, 1989.

Long, Max Freedom. *The Secret Science at Work*. Los Angeles, CA: Huna Research Publications, 1953.

MacKimmie, J. C. Hugh. *Presence of Angels: A Healer's Life*. Eureka, MT: Knowing Heart Publishing, 2005.

Manuchehri, Marie. *Intuitive Self-Healing*. Boulder, CO: Sounds True, 2012.

Mitchell, Stephen, ed. *Tao Te Ching*. New York: Harper & Row, 1991.

Mruk, Christopher J., and Joan Hartzell. *Zen and Psychotherapy*. New York: Springer Publishing, 2006.

Neill, Michael. *The Inside-Out Revolution*. Carlsbad, CA: Hay House, 2013.

Nisargadatta, Maharaj. *I Am That*. 1973. Reprint, Durham, NC: The Acorn Press, 1982.

Osborne, Arthur, ed. *The Teachings of Ramana Maharshi*. York Beach, ME: Samuel Weiser, 1996.

Pond, David. *Chakras for Beginners*. St. Paul, MN: Llewellyn, 1999.

Radin, Dean. *Entangled Minds: Extrasensory Experiences in a Quantum Reality*. New York: Paraview Pocket Books, 2006.

———. *Supernormal: Science, Yoga, and the Evidence for Extraordinary Psychic Abilities*. New York: Deepak Chopra Books, 2013.

Reps, Paul, comp. *Zen Flesh, Zen Bones*. Tokyo, Rutland, VT: C. E. Tuttle Co., 1957.

Rinpoche, Sogyal. *The Tibetan Book of Living and Dying*. San Francisco, CA: Harper, 1992.

Salzberg, Sharon. *Lovingkindness*. Boston, MA: Shambhala, 1997.

Shearer, Alistair, trans. and intro. *The Yoga Sutras of Patanjali*. New York: Bell Tower, 1982.

Singer, Michael A. *The Surrender Experiment*. New York: Harmony Books, 2015.

———. *The Untethered Soul*. Oakland, CA: New Harbinger Publications, 2007.

Smith, Huston. *And Live Rejoicing*. Novato, CA: New World Library, 2012.

Tolle, Eckhart. *The Power of Now*. Vancouver, Canada: Namaste Publishing, 2004.

Yogananda, Paramahansa. *The Art of Super Realization*. Los Angeles, CA: Yogoda Satsanga Society, 1930.

———. *The Autobiography of a Yogi*. Los Angeles, CA: Self-Realization Fellowship, 1956.

To Write to the Author

If you wish to contact the author or would like more information about this book, please write to the author in care of Llewellyn Worldwide Ltd. and we will forward your request. Both the author and the publisher appreciate hearing from you and learning of your enjoyment of this book and how it has helped you. Llewellyn Worldwide Ltd. cannot guarantee that every letter written to the author can be answered, but all will be forwarded. Please write to:

David Pond
⁄ Llewellyn Worldwide
2143 Wooddale Drive
Woodbury, MN 55125-2989

Please enclose a self-addressed stamped envelope for reply,
or $1.00 to cover costs. If outside the U.S.A., enclose
an international postal reply coupon.

Many of Llewellyn's authors have websites with additional information and resources. For more information, please visit our website at
www.llewellyn.com

GET MORE AT **LLEWELLYN.COM**

Visit us online to browse hundreds of our books and decks, plus sign up to receive our e-newsletters and exclusive online offers.

- **Free tarot readings • Spell-a-Day • Moon phases**
- **Recipes, spells, and tips • Blogs • Encyclopedia**
- **Author interviews, articles, and upcoming events**

GET SOCIAL WITH **LLEWELLYN**

Find us on
Facebook

Follow us on

www.Facebook.com/LlewellynBooks   www.Twitter.com/Llewellynbooks

GET BOOKS AT **LLEWELLYN**

LLEWELLYN ORDERING INFORMATION

Order online: Visit our website at www.llewellyn.com to select your books and place an order on our secure server.

Order by phone:
- Call toll free within the U.S. at 1-877-NEW-WRLD (1-877-639-9753)
- Call toll free within Canada at 1-866-NEW-WRLD (1-866-639-9753)
- We accept VISA, MasterCard, American Express and Discover

Order by mail:
Send the full price of your order (MN residents add 6.875% sales tax) in U.S. funds, plus postage and handling to: Llewellyn Worldwide, 2143 Wooddale Drive Woodbury, MN 55125-2989

POSTAGE AND HANDLING
STANDARD (U.S. & Canada):
(Please allow 12 business days)
$30.00 and under, add $4.00.
$30.01 and over, FREE SHIPPING.

INTERNATIONAL ORDERS:
$16.00 for one book, plus $3.00 for each additional book.

Visit us online for more shipping options. Prices subject to change.

FREE CATALOG!

To order, call
1-877-
NEW-WRLD
ext. 8236
or visit our
website

Over 100,000 Sold!

Chakras

For Beginners

A Guide to Balancing Your Chakra Energies

DAVID POND

Chakras for Beginners
A Guide to Balancing Your Chakra Energies
David Pond

You may think that difficult situations and emotions you experience are caused by other people or random events. This book will convince you that inner imbalance is not caused by situations in the outer world—instead, your imbalances create the situations that interfere with your sense of well-being and peace.

Chakras for Beginners explains how to align your energy on many levels to achieve balance and health from the inside out. In everyday terms, you will learn the function of the seven body-spirit energy vortexes called chakras. Practical exercises, meditations, and powerful techniques for working with your energy flow will help you overcome imbalances that block your spiritual progress.

- Discover colors and crystals that activate each chakra
- Explore the balanced and unbalanced expressions of each chakra's energies: survival, sexuality, power, love, creativity, intuition, and spirituality
- Practice spiritual exercises, visualizations, and meditations that bring your energies into balance

978-1-56718-537-9, 192 pp., 5 ³⁄₁₆ x 8   **$13.99**

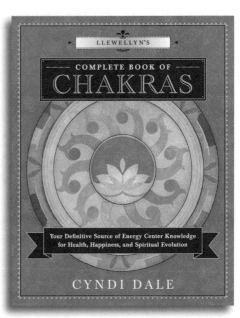

COMPLETE BOOK OF

CHAKRAS

Your Definitive Source of Energy Center Knowledge
for Health, Happiness, and Spiritual Evolution

CYNDI DALE

Llewellyn's Complete Book of Chakras
Your Definitive Source of Energy Center Knowledge for Health, Happiness, and Spiritual Evolution
Cyndi Dale

As powerful centers of subtle energy, the chakras have fascinated humanity for thousands of years. *Llewellyn's Complete Book of Chakras* is a unique and empowering resource that provides comprehensive insights into these foundational sources of vitality and strength. Discover what chakras and chakra systems are, how to work with them for personal growth and healing, and the ways our understanding of chakras has transformed throughout time and across cultures.

Lively and accessible, this definitive reference explores the science, history, practices, and structures of our subtle energy. With an abundance of illustrations and a wealth of practical exercises, Cyndi Dale shows you how to use chakras for improving wellness, attracting what you need, obtaining guidance, and expanding your consciousness.

978-0-7387-3962-5, 1056 pp., 8 x 10　　　　　　　**$39.99**